First published by Siboniso Thwala, 2020
Copyright © 2020 by Siboniso Thwala

ISBN 978-1-990962-30-1 (print)
ISBN 978-1-990962-31-8 (mobi)
ISBN 978-1-990962-32-5 (ePub)

Editor: Lara Katherine Stander
Proofreader: Kim Hunter
Cover Design and Typesetting: Gregg Davies Media
(www.greggdavies.com)

FINANCIAL REMEDY BY A BANKING ANALYST

Siboniso Thwala

*To the mother who raised me and stood by me
through all the difficult times;
These are my words of appreciation to you.*

*I have seen better days because of your love,
I have seen better things and times because of you,
I have conquered fear because of you,
I have learned to face adversity and take responsibility because of you,
Most importantly, I have learned to give God
control because of your values.*

*God knows how much you valued him, and I strongly believe that he knows
how you taught me to value him, and if by chance I ever choose to stray
away from him, it would never be because of you.*

*You always did your utmost because you appreciated
the value of hard work in this world.*

Thank you for Everything!

Martha Mafa Thwala: *Born 22 July 1957 - Died 17 June 2020*

May you Rest in Peace.

Thank you also to my wonderful family and the friends who have been there for me throughout the writing process and through various stages of my life.

Special mentions go to my close friend Modise Moaeng, who has been a good friend for as long as I can remember; Lara Katharine Stander, who has been a friend for ages and is also the editor of my books; Tiisetso Maloma, a fellow author who constantly provides guidance; Percy Nkuna, who has also been a wonderful friend for many years; Brian Majola (Buno), a singer and actor (currently starring in Rhythm City) who has been a friend since my high school days, and last but not least; Deborah Du Plooy from date with the Book, who has offered much guidance and mentorship throughout the process.

I'm stronger because of all your love and care!

ABOUT THE AUTHOR

SIBONISO THWALA IS AN AUTHOR, ANALYST, BANKER, ENTREPRENEUR AND COMMUNITY DEVELOPER

WRITING

His writing so far has focused on business management, entrepreneurship solutions and financial literacy and was inspired by the idea of leaving a legacy.

Quotes about writing:

> *"The best way to avoid making mistakes is to learn from the past, for the best way to live in the present with peace, is to have the knowledge of how to do it, and while living in the present and preparing for the future, one must be open to learning new things from other people"*
>
> — SIBONISO THWALA

Publications:

AUTOMOTIVE EXCELLENCE - EXPLORING THE INTUITIVE ART OF BUSINESS REPETITIVE EXCELLENCE

A book dedicated to those interested in business management, entrepreneurship and to those who want to improve sales, which was published in the year 2016.

A Financial Literacy self-help book published in the year 2020.

FINANCE, ANALYTICS AND BANKING CAREER

He began his career as a debt collector at MBD Attorneys (Munnik, Basson, Dagama) in 2005, while enrolled for his National Diploma in Banking at UNISA. He worked for approximately 2 years at MBD Attorneys.

He moved on in 2007 and became a manager for debt collections, at the age of 22 years, for one of the major banks in South Africa.

In 2010 he became interested in analytics and took up a role as a Business Intelligence Analyst. In 2014 he grew more interested in analytics and continued to grow this passion by expanding his experience with a change in focus; by specializing as a Product, Pricing and Profitability Analyst. In so doing, he remained in the Analytics world but took up an opportunity to become a Quantitative Analyst. Currently, he retains his role as a Quantitative Analyst in the banking sector.

His daily motivation for thriving in the Finance, Analytics and Banking career:

"Each day is a brand new day, with brand new opportunities to improve customer experiences, banking solutions and the business of banking and finance as a whole; I'm still chasing the day which brings me the opportunity to innovate and be quoted in the industry as, not only the man who brought the most profit to the industry, but also as the man who implemented the most comfortable financial journey for the bank customers."

ENTREPRENEURSHIP

As mentioned in his book, "**AUTOMOTIVE EXCELLENCE**", he became interested in the business world while still a teenager, in high school. He started his entrepreneurial career as a street vendor, selling his goods in trains and soccer stadiums.

Business initiatives:

2012 - ST DESKTOPS AND LAPTOPS

He ran a computer restoration and sales business where he bought broken computers, fixed them and then sold them; mostly to his target market of university students who wanted affordable computers. The skill of fixing computers was learned from a friend, he met in grade 10, who used to do it on a full-time basis to make a living. In 2014, with the spread of iPads and tablets, business profits slowed down as he didn't have the skill to fix them, so he decided to call it a day.

2014 – SiboCEE (SIBO COOKING AND EVENTS ENTERPRISE)

He bought his first mobile kitchen to provide catering at events and also to hire out cooking equipment for events such as funerals, weddings, parties and sports events. Later, in 2015, he expanded by starting up a fast-food tuck shop. Just as his business really started to thrive and grow, he went into partnership with someone who was helping him with building mobile kitchens. Unfortunately, the partnership didn't go well and he became extremely demotivated, but still wanted to give it another try; as quoted in his interview with the Mail and Guardian newspaper.

2018 – COOL EVENT

In 2018, he decided to grow in the events business. Although the SiboCEE business came with many challenges, he decided to stick to it and introduced additional services, adding an entertainment factor by hiring out sound systems. Check out more about Cool Event on Facebook.

REFERENCES

He was referenced in a book by his fellow writer and friend, Tiisetso Maloma, for providing creative solutions and objectivity which helped in finalizing the book, The Anxious Entrepreneur, which was released in 2015.

COMMUNITY DEVELOPMENT

He has initiated various community development projects in the past, and more especially after his first publication, as he has always been inspired by sharing knowledge and the idea of leaving his legacy.

KSE (Knowledge Sharing Enterprise) was started in this time. In 2017, he tried to convince a few people to form a partnership with him for this initiative, however he ended up continuing this journey with only one person; Sihle Picasso, a private chef, who had a slot on Kasi FM giving lessons on food and the culinary arts.

The MFBL (Mobile Food Business Lessons) which educated people on how to start and grow mobile food businesses was another of his initiatives, as quoted in the Daily Sun Newspaper.

Later, he also joined forces with Sebenzile, a radio station manager at Rainbow FM, to do more community work. This is where he began to do public speaking by engaging with young school young kids in Soweto.

Besides the MFBL, between 2017 and 2018, he has also done various public talk sessions, some of which were sponsored by the department of education; some of these talks were on financial literacy and others were based on his book, <u>Automotive Excellence</u>.

INTRODUCTION

The world as we knew it changed drastically in the year 2020, when it was hit by the pandemic known as COVID-19.

Within a few short months, this pandemic inflicted much pain and hardship, and forced major changes that the world has had no choice but to embrace. Many people have died, some have become orphans, others have lost their incomes due to the lockdowns (safety measures imposed by governments that have led to the closing of many companies), yet others have been forced to delay completing their qualifications and several have found themselves in even worse predicaments. Every one of us has been affected in some way by this pandemic, but those of us who survive it still stand a chance to be bold in the face of these new circumstances.

Don't however, read this book only if you are faced with difficulties because of COVID-19; even if you have not been financially impacted in any way, it is always a good thing to have information that might come in handy one day in the future.

Financial literacy plays a vital role in life because we are living in a world where almost everything we do requires the use of money. This book offers you not only an opportunity to find answers, but also gives some direction in achieving your goals to find peace and successful financial wellbeing.

CONTENTS

Chapter One

LESSON 1

- FINANCIAL GOALS AND OBJECTIVES

I'd like to kick-start this book with the topic of financial goals. The reason for this is that it will help you to decide if reading this book is worthy of your time. It should also help you to build an expectation of the message this book presents and ultimately, to know how to apply this information to your life. It is important to chase after goals because in the end they help us stand strong and, even in difficult times, to persist and look forward to tomorrow.

Setting goals is the first step in turning the invisible into the visible

— TONY ROBBINS

Globally, many people have become financially distressed due to the COVID-19 pandemic and it is therefore likely that some of them may be close to giving up on their financial aspirations. They might be overwhelmed and think that things will never get back to normal, and that all the efforts they have made in the past are now worthless. Due to this, some may even make drastic decisions that could have an even worse impact on their lives. So it is my hope that this chapter will help you to go back to the drawing board to revive your vision and rekindle your reason for living to the fullest each day you are blessed with.

During my journey in writing this book I tried, in many different ways, to define the term "FINANCIAL GOALS". While attempting to define the term, I did some research by questioning several people about what the term meant to them. What I discovered is that many people, in line with some of the searches I did on the internet, basically interpret the term in a way that highlights their financial wishes and dreams. So, since financial goals are close to people's wishes and dreams, it simply means that the term has different meanings for each individual.

However, even though the individual definitions of financial goals from my research relate to people's wishes and dreams, note that this is not one of those typical 'get rich quick' books that are commonly marketed in seminars with the promise to the readers that they will get rich when they finish reading the book; so if that is what you are looking for, then you are not looking in the correct place. It's simply a self-help book to give people some guidance on how they can deal with the financial difficulties they are currently facing, or might experience in the future, especially with the economy getting weaker.

If there is one true thing I could say about myself, even if held at gun point, it would be that I'm not interested in selling a get rich quick strategy; mostly because I don't perceive myself to be materialistic in that way. I can, however, guarantee that I have sufficient understanding to guide you towards some financial relief through my knowledge and experience in the financial arena.

In this book, I share my years of experience and a few tactics, learned by watching people who applied them to recover from the financial disasters they faced at some point in their lives.

My aim in writing this book is to help individuals who are interested in working towards building, or keeping, wealth and most importantly, who want to escape the day-to-day obstacles that hinder them from attaining their financial ambitions.

In a nutshell, this book is to help you to set your dreams in motion.

OBSTACLES TO FINANCIAL GOALS

Every journey is likely to have obstacles and a journey to financial stability is no different. As individuals, we constantly face distractions and in recent times, a huge obstacle has emerged in the form of COVID-19. Obstacles tend to slow down the fulfilment of our financial wishes and dreams and, more especially, our financial wellbeing. Consequently, this book is intended to help you achieve distraction-free financial goals.

While some people want to get rich, most people just want financial freedom and peace of mind. The common factor, however, between people who want to get rich and people who want financial freedom is that throughout the journey of achieving financial goals there will be obstacles. We need to realise, therefore, that what we are facing now is not the end, it's simply an obstacle, and in so doing we can free ourselves to set the objectives we need to achieve our goals.

DEFINE YOUR GOALS AND OBJECTIVES

Before delving too much further in this book, take a moment to brainstorm and then note down your financial goals by following the steps below. It is important for you to do this in order to make it easier for you to observe, and relate to, the topics discussed in this book and also to gain some ideas as to how you can apply the knowledge shared here to your personal life. Once the goals have been brainstormed, you will need to set objectives as to how you will achieve those goals. Objectives are actions, strategies or action plans that you will need to take in order to bring into being all the things that you deem necessary for your goals.

BRAINSTORM

BRAINSTORMING FINANCIAL GOALS STEP BY STEP

> *1. What are the most important things in your life*
> *right now?*

Note down the things you have and the things you need that you feel are necessary for your wellbeing. For example, you might have taken a pay cut due to reduced working hours, but it's still necessary for you to travel to work so that you can afford to pay for that degree you are working towards; or your medical insurance premium may have increased, but you still need to pay the premiums because it's vital for you and your loved ones to have access to medical treatment in case of illness or injury; or your business operating hours may have been reduced due to lockdown regulations imposed by the government as safety measures to reduce the spread of COVID-19, yet you still need to budget for accommodation because you and your loved ones can't be left without somewhere to live.

First, determine exactly what your basic needs are so that you don't lose sight of those things when establishing your goals. All the things that you identify as necessary in your life should be prioritised, because at some point, if you lack them, you will be at odds with your wellbeing and may find it more difficult to achieve your goals. If you don't make them a priority from the beginning they may forever be a hindrance to you in reaching your financial goals.

Next, set objectives as to which actions need to be taken to continue having these things in your life: would you consider compromising on your timetable for completing that degree, to cut your monthly fee obligations by reducing the number of courses that you enrol for per semester, or would you perhaps consider applying for funding from your employer or elsewhere? Alternatively, would you consider temporarily cutting down your entertainment budget to pay school fees?

These might not be the exact action plans you need to take but merely provide guidelines. You can take it further, and consult with other people for their opinions and guidance once you identify these priorities if you are still not sure what to do.

> *2. What are the things that would change your life for the worse if you did not have them?*

A good example of this may be that you are in arrears with your electricity bill. Your life would be affected negatively if your electricity supply was terminated. It would thus be time to prioritise payment of this bill and classify it in your brainstorming under financial goals.

These things, which might change your life for the worse if you didn't have them, might not only be things that will affect your life today or in the near future. They can also be things that might change your life in the far future if you didn't prioritise them now. An example of this could be a salary reduction; it would mean that you should focus on improving the situation because it will continue to trouble you and distract you from reaching your long term financial goals. The electricity bill is also just an example in this case, but things like this may become a distraction in the future because of accumulating interest and possibly taking longer to finish paying up that debt. The arrears might further distract you from reaching the front line of your savings goal regarding things like your retirement. If you often struggle to pay for essentials, look for alternatives: either reduce your use of the service or be upfront with the service provider, or creditor, and come up with a plan to sort out your payments, but we will explore more options about arrears in one of the following chapters.

3. Also, what are the things it would be better to let go of?

Keep in mind that there might be cause for some struggles; something making your life uncomfortable. What is it? (It could be anything - a problematic car that you must spend money repairing every month or owning a house that gets burgled a lot). You may need to consider a change to get rid of the things that are complicating your life. You need to face the truth and be honest with yourself when you look at things that if you didn't have them in your life, you might progress faster towards achieving your financial goals. In my days as a debt collector, I came across customers who were reluctant to even reduce their spending on unnecessary things, just because they were protecting their egos, but I've also seen customers who improved a lot financially, and got back on track with their financial goals, when they let go of the things that were not making their lives better. Once these objects have been identified, set arrangements as to how you will let go of them. Perhaps you should sell that car, stop using a credit card that has high interest charges and get rid of anything that decreases your quality of life.

4. What do you want to achieve soon?

It is important to keep this in mind to help you break down, step by step, how you will get to your ultimate goals. It will help you to number and sequence your goals. First things first. There are some things that you might need to achieve first in order for you to achieve others as, in some cases, things are linked to other things. For example; you might need to spend some money to fix the car that you identified as one of the things to let go of. Draw up an action plan as to how you would achieve this goal as quickly and simply as possible.

> *5. What do you want to see yourself achieving over a longer period, let's say in 5 years or more?*

What is your ultimate goal; the thing you wish most to achieve after all the time and effort spent on the above? What do you want, and where do you imagine yourself and your loved ones? Do you want to retire and travel the world, or do you want to own a business and take early retirement? All of the points above should help you to navigate towards this end; they might be the action plans for this ultimate goal as long as you brainstorm and then act on them.

Once you have determined your goals, write them down so that you can reflect on how each of the points discussed in this book relate to you and your situation.

SO NOW THE NEXT QUESTIONS ARE:

HOW DO I GET TO MY ULTIMATE GOAL
AND WHAT IF I GET DISTRACTED
WITHIN THE BRAINSTORMING EXERCISE?

HOW TO PROCEED AFTER GOAL SETTING

What is the quickest way to move from point A to point B?

What is the quickest way to achieving your goals?

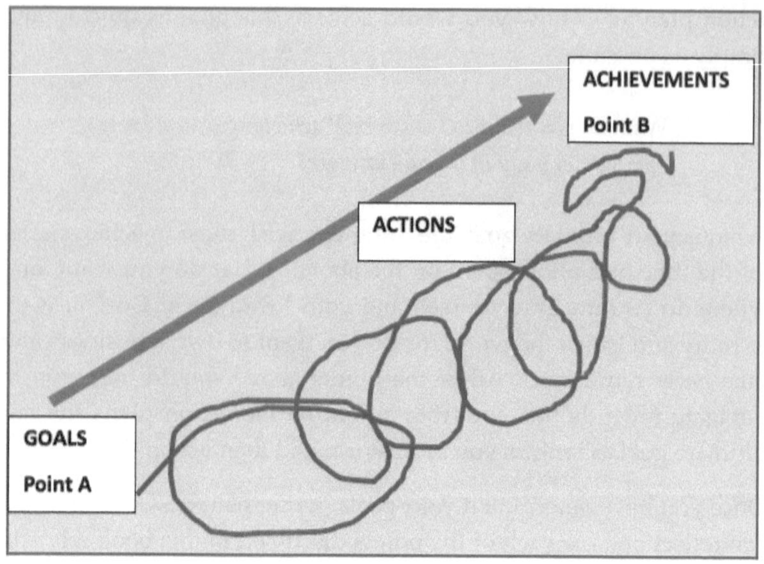

THE QUICKEST WAY IS THE STRAIGHT LINE

Now that you have set goals, be aware that the reality of life is that some things are just not attainable in a day and therefore may require constant repetition. It means that you have to be consistent in sticking to the plan in order to achieve the set goals.

For us to be successful in achieving our goals, we need to follow a pattern, or a sequence of actions which will ensure that we reach our goals. Now that's consistency. For example, you might need a longer period to materialise a goal. Without a doubt, to achieve your ultimate goal (as it's a vision for a longer period of time), you will need consistency over time and to put strict measures in place to achieve it. However, it doesn't necessarily mean that we need to constantly repeat the same behaviour, especially if we see that it's not contributing towards reaching the goal, or if we find obstacles along the way that impose a threat towards reaching the goal. Like now, with the world facing the effects of COVID-19, people have encountered hindrances and may need to adjust their action plans in order to achieve their goals.

WHAT IF YOU ARE IN A WRONG STRAIGHT LINE?

In some instances, you might find yourself in a pattern, or a line, that is not properly leading to the goal. Like for example, later in this book we explore various ways of avoiding spending a lot of money through avoiding unnecessary fees and optimizing on technology. Always keep in mind that the world of technology is a fast-moving world which requires people to constantly adapt to changes. Some of the changes brought about by COVID-19 have required people to adapt, especially to the use of technology.

In this instance, you need to identify an opportunity to switch between lanes; still within your chosen pattern of reaching your goal. There will often be instances where you may need to adjust your lane or pattern to one that is more effective.

WHAT'S NEXT?

How successful are financial goals without budgeting? Not that successful. So in the next chapter we will discuss a simple method of budgeting which might be complementary to your financial goals.

Chapter Two

LESSON 2

BUDGETING

Budgeting is the most vital part in planning how you will use or distribute your money. It is helpful in assisting you to determine whether you are able to afford to keep paying certain things, or have enough money to spend on needed or wanted items and also to predict if you will have enough money to put towards your future financial goals.

Try the 50/30/20 rule.

This record, called budgeting, is very important. We are living its philosophy on a daily basis, even if we do not physically plan it out, as we are eventually expected to make choices. What do you think happens when you go to the shop without a list and a predicted payment amount (previously budgeted from your side)? You end up making decisions to buy or not buy, based on your mental assessment of whether you have the means to buy.

A budget also needs consistent management and periodic review according to your changing circumstances. Everyone's budget varies according to their needs.

A good principle to follow is the "50/30/20 rule" which is discussed in a book titled, "All Your Worth: The Ultimate Lifetime Money Plan," by Elizabeth Warren and Amelia Warren Tyagi.

DISCUSSING THE PRINCIPLE

The 50% is for your needs

This refers to 50% of your take-home income.

It includes things like your shelter, transport, school fees, food, medical bills (not your medical aid deductions), and other things that are vital to your day to day survival.

The best thing about this is that if you stick strictly to the targeted 50%, you are more likely to cut down on less important needs if you cannot afford to maintain them.

Ok, it might sound obvious, but pay attention; some needs are more expensive than other needs. Accommodation, for example, is a basic need but there are expensive accommodations and affordable accommodations.

If the accommodation in which you are currently living costs more than 50% of your take-home income, then you should try to find one that would be within your 50% budget.

The 30% is for your wants

Wants are not needs in that you can do without them if you cannot afford them. Things like: going to a bar to drink and relax with friends, or the latest smart phone (especially when you still have a perfectly good phone), or the amazing new convertible vehicle that everyone has been talking about, or even a dream holiday at a seaside resort.

Having said this, we all know that wants are important; no-one wants to work day in and day out just to pay for vital needs, so allocating this 30% to your wants would act as a guideline to properly manage your finances. Imagine how having this as a goal could encourage you to work hard and manage your money if you love to go on holidays. If you knew for a fact that the cost of your desired holiday would be more than you could afford, even with a budget; you would work harder, and plan ways to earn even more income so that you could eventually reach the point where it would be affordable.

The 20% is for your savings

Savings, Savings, Savings!!

This is not easy; it's the most difficult part of the rule to follow, especially with so many temptations around us. But it is important to save on a regular basis, mainly so that you have something to fall back on in an emergency situation.

Having savings can help in many ways, such as:

- starting a new business;
- paying for emergencies such excess on your insurance;
- paying for the funeral of a family member who had no funeral cover;
- paying for school events like a weekend camp or overseas trip for your child.

Your savings can also be utilised to satisfy your wants, like going on holiday. The reality is that most of us need to save our money on a monthly basis in order to afford to go away for a week or two. Whether it's to a resort or a trip abroad, only your savings can help you do that. The more you save, the quicker you are able to have your holiday.

This budget rule is very useful as a guide and if it can help you to set targets and motivate you to do more, then it's a wonderful tool in reaching your goals.

BENEFITS OF USING THIS BUDGETING RULE

Note again that this budget rule is applicable to your income after tax, or your basic take-home salary. What this rule does is, very simply, is to encourage an individual to measure their income and then to structure the spending of it.

It is very useful because it encourages you to save and spend according to your income so that when you get a salary increase, you will automatically be motivated to revise your budget according to your new income so as to increase the amount you are able to save.

It's a simple-to-follow guideline for individuals. It helps them to set their financial targets and personal development plans, and is also a way to further encourage them, where necessary, to plan ways to make more income to better satisfy their needs, wants and savings requirements.

AN EXAMPLE / STRUCTURE OF THE 50/30/20 BUDGETING RULE

This is just a guideline to assist you in creating your own ideal 50/30/20 budget. In this demonstration we'll use a monthly earning figure of R12 000.00

50/30/20 BUDGET EXAMPLE TEMPLATE

Salary / Income	12000		
NEEDS		**Needs** (50% of your take home income) 5950	50%
Accommodation	2500		
Car	1000		
Insurance	500		
School Fee	400		
Food	800		
Petrol	500		
Data, Cellular, Clothing, other accounts	250		
WANTS		**Wants** (30% of your take home income) 3650	30%
Concert Ticket	200		
Decoration for New Kitchen	350		
School Trip	600		
New Clothes	400		
Outing with friends	400		
New Hair Style	400		
New TV for the Bedroom	1300		
SAVINGS		**Savings** (20% of your take home income) 2350	20%
Savings account	500		
Retirement Investment	1000		
Savings for December Trip	850		

CLOSING

If you are a person that has survived till now without a proper budget, you can start by making adjustments to and reducing your unnecessary wants and needs. Then increase the priority of saving so that if you can afford to save more, you do it.

For your further information, if you didn't already know this: savings are not only good for you as a person, they are also good for the overall economy in your country, because the more the population within an economic system saves, the more funds are available for banks to lend out money to generate more jobs by helping people start new businesses.

It's important to review your budget every month, and also for you to keep track of your spending on little things, because it's usually those little things that distract you from sticking to your budget. For example: you may decide to buy a R100.00 meal from a restaurant because you are too tired to cook for the evening. There is no harm in that, unless it becomes a habit that distracts you from your budget. Sometimes you lose track of that R100.00 because often in your mind it seems as if it's a once-off expenditure; but if it becomes a repetitive once-off, that occurs two or three times a week, it becomes a problem.

When creating your budget, remember to prioritize your needs first. (Make sure to cater for insurance premiums when you are looking at your needs).

Your past debt obligations should also form part of your budget under needs. You need to ensure that you pay your debts so that you can be free and stay out of trouble.

It is also important to include a Retirement investment in your budget. Many people waste their income until it's too late. They let other needs supersede this, forgetting the reality that becoming old and unable to work, is an inevitable fact of life. The sooner you start to treat your retirement investment as a non-negotiable need; the better off you will be when you arrive at that point. Most financial institutions offer options and products that can help with regards to that type of investment.

Chapter *Three*

LESSON 3

ALIENATE OR BEFRIEND THE CREDIT REPORT

I f there is one thing that I feel was neglected in the past as part of our basic education, whether under life skills or personal finance lessons, it is the credit report.

Throughout my career, I learnt a lot about credit reports and most of those things I wish I had learned earlier, at least as early as high school, in order to prepare me for the reality of the credit and lending world.

A credit report is a summary of an individual's credit activity. In basic terms, it is a record of how committed you are to honouring your debt obligations, as well as how you are utilising the credit available to you in the market. Creditors submit this information to the credit bureaus on a monthly basis, so that they have access to a public record of how well you conduct your payments and how often you take up debt. The main purpose of the credit report is to try to keep you from accumulating debt that you cannot afford to pay, although many people still think that it is just another way for creditors to mess up your life and punish you. A person who maintains a good credit report and handles their finances responsibly however, should seldom if ever, have any problems with creditors.

CREDIT SCORING

A credit report has score points which summarise and reflect your financial activities.

Score ranges:

- 550 = perceived as bad
- 550 – 649 = perceived poor
- 650 – 699 = perceived as fair
- 700 – 749 = perceived as good
- 750 – above = perceived as excellent

*The ranges above may be subject to change.

THINGS THAT AFFECT YOUR CREDIT SCORING

- Payment history (24 month period. Any missed payments thus reflect for 2 years)
- Amount you owe vs. what you earn
- Scope or period size of the report
- The kinds of credit that you take up
- Credit enquiries

WHAT YOU NEED TO KNOW TO IMPROVE YOUR CREDIT SCORE

Sometimes in life things get broken. Even your credit score could be in a situation where once it was wonderful and now it's not. Well, we all go through rough times, this is life after all! So in cases where you find yourself having taken a wrong turn, here are a few tips to help you get back on the right track.

- Having no credit history can be limiting

For individuals like you and me, to prove that we are worthy of being given a loan or credit facility, especially by a financial institution, it is important to have some kind of credit history. A record of how much credit you have taken up and how committed you have been to reducing it, plays a very important role in determining whether creditors should, or should not, give you a loan. Getting, and paying off, a clothing account might be a good way to start building a record.

- Making payments on time

Approximately a third or more of your credit score reflects your ability to keep your promises to make regular payments on time. Most debts are paid monthly, so when you honour your monthly payment obligations on or before the payment due date, you score easy credit points.

- Don't get into a position where creditors are forced to resort to court orders

Having adverse information such as non-payment or late payments on your record can negatively affect your credit score, but court orders are a lot worse. Please keep in mind that any court orders granted against you may take years to remove from your credit profile. Judgement orders especially may take several years to remove from your record, depending on the type of debt. It is therefore essential to avoid getting into a position where summonses, judgements and attachments are noted on your credit report.

- Keep your personal debt limits as low as possible

For your credit report to be favourable, you should not have to utilise more than a third of your salary to pay debt. Note that not just your salary, but also your available funds after payment commitments, is always assessed to determine how creditworthy you are.

- Amount utilised vs. available credit limit should be kept as low as possible

This rule follows from the one above in that you should not allow yourself to become overextended. Creditors should always check the ratio of what your current manageable limit is within the total limit of a third of your salary. If you use more, it often means that you are likely to be struggling to keep up your lifestyle on your salary. Basically it means that you can barely manage to survive on your income.

- Close accounts not used

Decide which accounts to close once you are no longer using them. Having too many accounts also limits your available credit. Now why would you limit yourself because of accounts that you are not even using?

- Limit credit enquiries

Credit enquiries are done by creditors when you apply for credit and often also if your account goes into arrears. These enquiries are performed to check the number of accounts that you have and how you are paying these accounts.

Every enquiry is recorded on your credit report and they have a negative impact on your overall credit score. The more credit enquiries you have, the more they impact your score. The enquiries reduce your credit score by 5-10 points and they reflect on your report for 2 years.

Note that some enquiries may be disputed in cases where permission was not given to a creditor to run one (this does not apply in arrear cases).

What you need to understand is that when creditors phone to offer you products you don't need, it's not necessary for you to check if you qualify financially if you don't intend taking up the product. I experienced instances in the past where telesales consultants phoned me to offer a product and when I told them that I was not in the market for that product, some of them insisted that I check, or tried to bait me into checking whether I could afford the product offered, in the hope that I would change my mind and take up the product after verifying that I could afford it. In these instances, I would always tell them not to proceed with the enquiry, because that enquiry would be recorded on my credit profile as if I was attempting to get credit for a product or service. This is still recorded as an enquiry even if not taken up, so you need to be careful as it may eventually negatively affect your credit rating.

- Don't rob Peter to pay Paul

If you owe a debt and wish to pay it off, don't borrow from another creditor in order to pay off that debt. This will indicate that you are settling one debt with another and this also has a negative impact on your credit report.

There are, however, some acceptable options should it benefit you and all the relevant parties. One such option is debt consolidation, whereby you merge all your debt into one account and therefore only have to focus on paying one large amount instead of many small ones. (If this option is considered, it is extremely important to ensure that the interest rate of the debt consolidation loan does not exceed what you would have previously paid on the smaller debts.)

- Avoid revolving loans

Revolving credit is a type of credit whereby the credit available to you is automatically renewed when the amount due is paid off. The danger is that there is no fixed number of payments specified on a revolving credit loan and your repayment amount is often worked out on the full amount of the loan, even should you only withdraw a portion of it. Also, this kind of debt normally has a high interest rate charge and will negatively impact your credit score.

- Check your credit report

Even if you are not applying for any loans, it is a good habit to check your credit report from time to time to make sure that the information on the report is correct and you are aware of all the accounts reflecting thereon.

You may subscribe with some of the credit bureaus to receive a monthly report, and/or alerts that inform you when there is a new notation added under your name.

THE ACTUAL MEANING OF A CREDIT REPORT

You can only consume anything to a limited extent. This is because sometimes you run out of the power to continue to consume after exercising your power too much!

Further on in the book, Lesson 9 (Avoid Bad Beginnings) is aimed mainly at those readers who are still new to employment. By leveraging off of that chapter, I would like to explain bad beginnings further and refer to "POWER".

The score that you see on your credit report is not only a number, but also your buying power or ability to spend! In economics, there is a term which refers to how hungry one is to consume and how powerful one is to consume still more. This term is: "Propensity to consume".

To explain this in simple terms, let's say that one afternoon you are hungry and decide to buy lunch, so you buy an eight piece fried chicken meal. You eat all eight pieces and feel less hungry than before you started eating. In the interim, your friend has bought sixteen pieces of chicken and asks you to join him for lunch to share his meal. He eats his full share of eight pieces, but you can only manage three. Your power to consume has thus decreased because you already ate eight pieces and therefore cannot eat another eight.

In the same way, your credit score reflects your power to take up more credit, as well as your ability to service that credit according to contractual agreement. When you take on more credit your score is impacted and thus indicates that your power to pay off the credit has decreased. Should you then default on those debts it gets even worse, because it shows that you no longer have the power to service your credit agreements.

If you are one of those people who are spending a lot of their monthly income paying off inflated debt because you are not aware of how much your credit score might help you pay a lower interest rate, this advice should give you the confidence to approach a trusted bank instead of going to a micro-lender out of desperation.

Your credit score will always guide you as to how much you can afford, and expect to spend on your debt. So if you do your homework before applying for a loan, you could save yourself a lot of stress in the long run.

CLOSING

Your credit report and your budget go hand in hand, so if you want to live a well-structured and less stressful life, it would be wise to monitor these two things carefully on a regular basis.

Chapter Four

LESSON 4

HANDLING BAD DEBTS

WHAT ARE BAD DEBTS (ARREARS)?

Bad debt occurs when a debtor fails to meet his/her contractual agreement, or agreements with a lender (e.g. financial institution), in that his/her monthly payments (or instalments) are not up to date. Thus when someone fails to meet his/her contractual agreements in the form of regular monthly payments, he or she is classified as a bad debtor or a bad payer. Basically it is a breach of contract according to law, to put it in simple terms and to paint a clear definition in your mind.

At the beginning of my career, I worked for an attorney firm collecting bad debts, so in this chapter I will share with you things I witnessed during that time, so that you can learn from other people's mistakes.

Those days were bitter-sweet but I learned a lot. The experience helped me a great deal in my endeavours thereafter, but came with a lot of emotional and verbal abuse from the customers. Do I blame them? No, I don't! Actually, I forgive them because I understand that most of them felt cornered by difficult times.

The feeling of losing control over your finances is one of the most terrible feelings that one can ever have, whether you are a family man, or a single person who is trying to build a future. For many people, financial problems can trigger a huge set-back in their lives and the lives of those that are dependent on them because it's emotionally stressful. Some people are even driven as far as committing suicide when cornered by debt. Others make drastic decisions such as resigning from work in order to get their pension fund paid out, with the hope that they will pay off their debts and then get another job, while not even having a promise of further employment at the time of resignation. This happens because being in arrears plays with our emotions, but we will explore a little about money and emotions in one of the following chapters.

For now, let me take you through my journey and share with you what I discovered during all the years that I worked in the debt-collections space. If you are currently facing a situation where you are in arrears, or in breach of your obligations, I hope that my experiences will help you to find a solution.

THE JOURNEY AND THE DISCOVERY

Like most jobs, in my first job as a debt collector I had to attend training for the first two weeks. The training comprised of product knowledge, details about the types of accounts that we would be collecting on, the ethics of debt-collection, various regulations and most importantly, the legal process of collecting on debts.

Then, on my first actual work day after the training, I was exposed to a typical day in a debt-collection environment; it was a Friday in the summer of 2005.

Because I was working for a law firm as a debt collector, the thing that stood out for me on my first day, despite having learned it during training, was that when an agent (debt collection agent or attorney) is involved in collecting debts as a third party, an account is no longer perceived to be in good standing. In other words, the debtor is perceived by the creditor to no longer be a good customer. This is the stage where a creditor will resort to engaging third party collections agents or attorneys to collect the debt.

One of the first things that I noticed was that the collectors in that office were frustrated; there was tension in the environment. But why was there tension in the environment?

As the days passed, I realized that there was tension because it was not an easy task for collectors to keep phoning people asking for payment, especially when most of the debtors had reasons for not being able to pay. There were many reasons that made people unable to meet their obligations. I found that the majority of the people we called couldn't meet their debt obligations because of unexpected events such as a death in the family, retrenchment, being medically boarded or being over-committed on their monthly debt repayments (i.e. spending more than they could afford).

For some of them, being in arrears could have been prevented if they had budgeted properly, paid more attention to their credit score, and possibly if they had had a little bit of extra information about financial literacy, like that provided in this book. Most of the reasons for being in arrears, or being in breach of financial obligations, arise when we drop the ball, or become lax on the small things in our budgets. Preparing for unforeseen circumstances or emergencies with insurance payments as part of your budget, could save you a lot of trouble later. See lesson 2, where we speak about the 50/30/20 budget rule, and include insurance in your "needs" column.

OTHER CRUCIAL FACTORS THAT CAUGHT MY ATTENTION DURING THE JOURNEY

THIRD PARTY FEES

When your account is handed over to a third party for collection, there are likely to be fees incurred in relation to the debt that is owed.

- The collections agent may have the right to charge individually for all the services rendered to the creditor. For example, if the debt collections agent attempts to contact you by phone, they can charge a fee for the telephone call.
- If the debt collections agent sends you a letter regarding payment of your debt, the creditor is permitted to debit your account with the cost incurred by sending you the letter.

Letters and/or legal documents that may be issued are as follows:

- Letter of Demand (LOD)
- Summons (Writ of Foreclosure)
- Default or Summary Judgement Notice
- Writ of Attachment (Warrant of Execution against Property)

INTEREST

- Over and above the due balance amount as at date of foreclosure (i.e. the hand over amount as at the date when a debt collection agent becomes involved), the monthly interest charges will accumulate and continue to increase the debt. Additionally, the collection fees for services rendered to the creditor will be added to the account of the debtor thus increasing the debt even further. The balance will thus increase inclusive of all these fees: the initial balance amount at hand over, service fees and compound interest.
- Compound interest is simply interest on top of interest. I remember from my days of being a debt collector that this was often difficult to explain to debtors, simply because of the traditional way of explaining this term, so let me explain this to you in a fashion other than the popular or traditional way.

- When an account is being handed over for collection, the balance due increases faster than when the account is in a normal state; meaning that a bad debt account accumulates more fees than when the account is in good standing.

- Often during the process of collection by the collections agent, disputes arise over the amounts owed to the creditor. The cause for these disputes is typically confusion between simple interest and compound interest.

SIMPLE INTEREST

Simple interest is basically a single fixed interest amount calculated on an initial fixed principal amount. For example, if you borrow an amount of R12,000.00 (Capital amount) at an interest rate of 5% payable, your total interest will be R600.00; if you pay this over a period of 12 months your monthly payment will be fixed at R1,050.00 until the debt is paid. This means that the total interest charged is a fixed amount added onto your repayment of the borrowed amount. Although a monthly repayment is the most common, how the interest is paid will depend on the agreement made between the lender and the borrower.

COMPOUND INTEREST

Compound interest is interest charged on both the original loan amount as well as subsequent interest charged over the loan period. Thus when the capital or original loan amount is R12, 000.00, the 5% interest will be charged periodically (whether it's monthly, yearly or quarterly); so at the end of the first period interest will be charged on the principal amount, thereafter for each subsequent period, interest will be charged on the balance outstanding (which will be inclusive of the interest charged on the previous period).

Compound interest rewards those who pay extra, over and above the required instalments, but penalises those who do not meet their obligations. The table below illustrates this by comparing three debtors who borrowed the same amount at the same interest over the same loan period: R12, 000.00 at 5% over 12 Months.

Debtor 1 (Oliver Q) pays an additional R1000.00 every month and so clears his debt in 6 months, thus saving himself almost R400.00 in interest. Total interest paid = R208.07.

Debtor 2 (John D) pays exactly what is required every month to clear his debt in 12 months. Total interest paid = R600.00

Debtor 3 (Tommy M) makes little or no payment resulting not only in additional interest charges but legal fees on his account. Legal costs = R7800.00. Total Interest on settlement = R2, 622.97; (*note this is worked out on the basis of payment being made at the end of the 12month period). This is a worst case scenario and would differ if any token payments were made. It just gives basic idea of how badly things can go wrong if we fail to meet our financial commitments.

***Note that legal charges in the table do not reflect the actual fees currently charged by legal practitioners and/or financial institutions.*

	Oliver Q	Interest	Payment	Balance	John D	Interest	Payment	Balance		Tommy M	Interest	Payment	Balance
01-Jan	12,000.00	50.00		12,050.00	12,000.00	50.00		12,050.00	01-Jan	12,000.00	50		12,050.00
			2,050.00	10,000.00			1,050.00	11,000.00				0.00	12,050.00
01-Feb		45.45		10,045.45		50.00		11,050.00	01-Feb		54,77		12,104.77
			2,045.45	8,000.00			1,050.00	10,000.00				0.00	12,104.77
01-Mar		40.00		8,040.00		50.00		10,050.00	01-Mar		60,52		12,165.29
									LOD	300.00			12,465.29
			2,040.00	6,000.00			1,050.00	9,000.00				0.00	12,465.29
01-Apr		33.33		6,033.33		50.00		9,050.00	01-Apr		69,25		12,534.54
			2,033.33	4,000.00			1,050.00	8,000.00				0.00	12,534.54
01-May		25.00		4,025.00		50.00		8,050.00	01-May		78,34		12,612.88
									Summons	2000.00			14,612.88
			2,025.00	2,000.00			1,050.00	7,000.00				612.88	14,000.00
01-Jun		14.29		2,014.29		50.00		7,050.00	01-Jun		100		14,100.00
			2,014.29	0.00			1,050.00	6,000.00				0.00	14,100.00
01-Jul				0.00		50.00		6,050.00	01-Jul		117,5		14,217.50
									Judgment	1000.00			15,217.50
				0.00			1,050.00	5,000.00				0.00	15,217.50
01-Aug				0.00		50.00		5,050.00	01-Aug		152,18		15,369.68
				0.00			1,050.00	4,000.00				0.00	15,369.68
01-Sep				0.00		50.00		4,050.00	01-Sep		192,12		15,561.80
									Attachment	3000.00			18,561.80
				0.00			1,050.00	3,000.00				0.00	18,561.80
01-Oct				0.00		50.00		3,050.00	01-Oct		309,36		18,871.16
				0.00			1,050.00	2,000.00				0.00	18,871.16
01-Nov				0.00		50.00		2,050.00	01-Nov		471,78		19,342.94
				0.00			1,050.00	1,000.00				0.00	19,342.94
01-Dec				0.00		50.00		1,050.00	01-Dec		967,15		20,310.09
									Sale	1500.00			21,810.09
				0.00			1,050.00	0.00				21,810.09	0.00
			208.07			600.00				7800.00	2,622.97		

In a majority of cases in the current market, the interest charged on loans is compound interest. Apart from interest, the major contributing factors that negatively affect people's financial status when an account is handed over for collection are the following:

- Service fees for collection of the debt,

- Costs added for Letters or statements sent out by the collections agent,

- Telephone calls,

- Tracing fees,

- Legal fees.

Besides the financial aspect, however, it is also important to note the negative effects of arrears on a debtor's credit record. Most debts incurred by a person, whether they be from a financial institution or a retailer, are listed on the national credit bureau. This allows any entity to whom a person makes application for credit, access to the applicant's financial record. All defaults are listed from month one and remain on record for a period of at least a year. Court Judgments remain on record for a period of five years from the date they are granted, but are valid in court for a period of up to thirty years as long as all criteria of the NCA (National Credit Act) are met.

WHY DO PEOPLE END UP OVER-INDEBTED?

One of the duties I had to perform while serving as an analyst for a bank was to drill down to the fundamental reasons for why many clients are unable to pay their loans. Keeping in mind that the function of an analyst is to analyse data in order to find solutions to problems within an industry at any particular time, my duty at that stage, was to find answers as to why more and more people were falling into debt that they could not afford. Reasons included being over-indebted due to lack of proper planning, not following a budget and lack of education with regards to financial matters.

Another major factor I discovered during this study however, was simply a factor of human nature. Many people simply avoided the issue instead of crying for help when they found themselves approaching tough times.

If it happens that now, as you are reading this book, you find yourself in a similar position, don't wait until it's too late to ask for help but rather look at some of the tips below and apply them to your situation.

TIPS FOR SURVIVING ARREARS

PROACTIVENESS AND HONESTY

Honesty, with yourself as well as your creditors, is important to your survival during bad financial circumstances: "The truth shall set you free!"

Bad debts are not the end of your world; there's always a way to stay in the good books of your creditors.

If you can no longer afford to pay the required instalment for your debt, speak up before it's too late. I've seen many people who show signs of financial pressure wait until it's too late. Instead of taking the initiative, they wait until the creditor contacts them to establish their reasons for non-payment and to prompt them to make payment. In many cases, those clients were able to see the signs that their finances were moving in the wrong (problematic) direction, but ended up in denial, desperately hoping that a plan would materialise out of nowhere to solve their problems.

Alternatively, should you decide to face the problem and request assistance early on, you may be surprised by the willingness of your creditors to offer various possible options to help you, before you accumulate arrears on your account. A creditor would often be willing to assist you in making a special payment arrangement if you show a willingness to cooperate with them in finding an affordable solution. I observed many devastating failures while working in a home loans environment, where people lost their houses due to a lack of honesty with themselves - cases that could have had a much more positive outcome had those clients been less deceitful and more cooperative. Most of the bigger financial institutions offer unique client rescue packages, which can be tailored to assist individuals with their unique struggles, but most often those who get rescued are those who realise and accept early on that they need help. It is counterproductive to wait until your account is in arrears to approach the creditor for help, especially if you can foresee the problems and hard times.

Always draft your budget before you get your salary. The budget will help you to establish whether you are living within your means or outside of them because, just as we have a need to keep breathing to function, we also have other needs and some of the financial needs we have are because of unexpected events that we encounter. Therefore, maintaining a budget will give you a good idea of whether you are managing to live your normal life within the parameters of your monthly income. It is a good way to identify problems, or potential problems early. So even when you identify that you are struggling to manage, there is no need to worry because identifying problems sooner rather than later, gives you the advantage of attempting to negotiate with your creditor while time is still on your side. Concluding an arrangement for a payment holiday or for a special payment arrangement, without defaulting or skipping a payment, may prevent you from being listed as a defaulter on the credit bureau systems. The best option when anticipating a tough period is to contact your credit provider and make them aware of the situation. You may be surprised at the amount of help available to you just by talking to a qualified person about your situation.

Don't make promises you cannot keep. It's good to be hopeful and positive, but it's also dangerous to rely on projected income where there is no confirmation or certainty. Often people find themselves in deep and challenging financial situations because they have banked on receiving money in the future. For example, I've dealt with people who have made debt a month before their salary increase is confirmed, based on the expectation of receiving a decent increase, but then run into problems because they don't get what they expected. I've seen bank clients promise to pay their full arrears, or clear all their debts, based on the hope of getting a decent bonus payment that does not materialise or is less than expected.

They end up being disappointed and frustrated and not able to meet their financial obligations. I've also seen business owners, who spend money on the assumption of receiving lucrative work and good contracts, lose everything they've previously achieved. Taking risks is not always a bad thing, and can be beneficial, but it's a lot safer to do your homework and make decisions based on confirmed income. I'm not trying to limit you in any way; I'm merely attempting to awaken your sense of reality.

SOD

SOD is an acronym which stands for Substitution of Debtor. This may apply in cases where you have a joint debt account with someone else. Most commonly, joint loans are taken by married people when they buy a house together. As an example, let's fast forward to a few years after the house was purchased. The marriage has failed and the couple is now in a position where they can no longer live in the same house. They may come to an agreement that one party will retain ownership of the house and become solely liable for payments of the instalments going forward. However, such an agreement between parties, even if it is part of a divorce agreement, is not sufficient from a legal perspective. The creditor must be advised that the loan contract needs to be amended. This can be done by applying for an SOD. Should an SOD be approved by the creditor, one of the account holders will be removed completely from the contract and the debt will no longer appear on the credit profile of that person.

It's important for you to know, however, that an SOD is not automatically granted once a formal request is submitted. The creditor will first need to do a full credit assessment on the party who wishes to take over the debt in their sole capacity, in order to assess whether they will be able to continue paying the debt without the involvement of the other party.

DEBT COUNCELLING

Debt counselling is another possible solution to help you through difficult times, provided that you act before it's too late.

Definition according to Wikipedia:

> *"Credit counselling (known in the United Kingdom as Debt counselling) is commonly a process that is used to help individual debtors with debt settlement through education, budgeting and the use of a variety of tools with the goal to reduce and ultimately eliminate debt."*

Reflection and a play-back of memories from my own experiences:

In July 2008, I was tasked to oversee clients who were going under debt review and discovered that the number of people going under debt review was growing tremendously. I couldn't fully understand the reasons for that at the time, but now thinking back, I don't blame those poor people. Debt review had become the "in thing", but it was understandable due to the harsher lending policies which South Africa had introduced. Debt review was a new mechanism introduced into the economy at the time, with the aim of assisting the public to survive through the recession, since previously this kind of assistance was sorely lacking in the system.

Many people fell badly into arrears and this scared them into opting for debt review. For the majority of them though, this could have been prevented had they managed their credit and spending behaviours correctly.

When you approach a debt counsellor, he or she will request that you provide all your credit agreements and a monthly income and expenditure statement. Based on this information he/she will assess whether you qualify to go under the debt review process. Should you indeed be over-indebted to the point that you cannot afford to pay your debt with your monthly income, he/she will then calculate a payment plan around what is affordable for you and thereafter negotiate agreements with each of your creditors to pay a percentage of the instalment for each debt. Once this is concluded, an application will be made to court to make the restructured payment plan an order of court. Every month you will then pay a consolidated sum to the debt counsellor. Upon receipt of your funds, the debt counsellor will distribute payments to all of your creditors according to the terms of agreement.

*note that there will be fees due to the debt counsellor, as well as legal fees for the court order, which will be included in your monthly repayment.

Should you choose this option, you need to be aware of the following: as with everything in life, there are unscrupulous people who are on the hunt to take advantage of people in desperate situations. I came across many of these during my years of service working in the debt collection space.

One such example was Thabang (not his real name), who became a debt counsellor because he realised that he could take advantage of the fact that many people were struggling to pay their debts during a time when the overall economy in the country was at an all-time low. Due to the bad economic climate of that time, he discovered that it would be easy for him to get into debt counselling as a profession. Once he had the certificate, it was simple to take on uninformed people as clients. Desperate people who paid fees they could not afford for a service that was not delivered and eventually ended up in a worse situation than before applying for debt counselling.

The most important thing about debt counselling is that it should help you get out of debt. So, although there are now much stricter criteria in place for becoming a debt counsellor, you should always be very careful in ensuring that whoever you go to for financial assistance has your best interests at heart.

The benefits of going under debt review are as follows:

- Under debt review, your monthly /contractual instalment amount is reduced to an amount that you are more able to afford and constitutes one single payment as opposed to many separate payments.
- The purpose of debt counselling is to assist you to finish paying your debt in an affordable way, in the shortest possible time.
- Creditors cannot institute legal action, or further legal action, against you unless you default on the debt review agreement.

SURRENDERING

Another option of which people might not be aware (which I'm not putting to you as advice but merely as something I've seen people do in desperate times), is getting out of debt by choosing to cede a life-policy. Some people, when applying for a mortgage bond, hand over ownership of their life cover to the bank as security against the loan. The bank then becomes the owner of the policy (cessionary) thus, in the event that you pass away or lose an income, the insurance will first pay the creditor the money owed to them before paying out any other amounts. If a person does decide to make use of this option, they should first consult with a financial advisor to give them a detailed explanation of the consequences of the decision and must then also not forget to read the fine print carefully.

SOME TIPS TO HELP YOU TO FINISH PAYING YOUR DEBTS AND SAVE ON INTEREST

- Round up your payments if you can afford it.

For example; if your instalment is R360.00 per month you can simply round up this payment to R400.00 per month, which will help you to save on the interest and also to pay off the debt before the expected time.

- Consolidate your debt.

A Consolidation loan should be useful for saving on interest. Compare the interest rates that you are paying on all your micro loans versus what you might pay for one consolidation loan. If you have debts with micro-lenders, or even loan sharks, the interest that you are paying is likely to be excessive, so taking up a consolidation loan is an alternative you may wish to consider.

- Sell some things that you no longer use or need.

There is no good reason to hold on to things that are not useful to you. Unless something has serious sentimental value, it would benefit you to sell it and use the money to pay off your debts.

- Sell your leave days.

Some employers allow you to liquidate excess leave days if you have accumulated a certain amount. As long as you take the minimum required leave every year, you should be entitled to sell some of your accumulated leave days to the company in order to settle your debts.

- Set up a fixed debit order.

Should you make a decision to pay an extra amount on your monthly payment, set up a fixed debit order for that amount. This will take away the temptation to default on your decision. A debit order helps you to stay disciplined as it goes off on the specified date, with the instructed amount every month without you having to worry about it.

- Pay all your creditors via debit order.

As mentioned above, using debit orders to make payment saves you the effort of having to physically make the payment every month thus keeping you out of the temptation to use the funds on other things.

- Alternatively, set up a stop order payment.

Nowadays it's very easy to set up a stop order. Just go to your banking app or internet banking to set up a scheduled payment.

* note that a debit order instruction is issued to your bank from your creditor, whereas a stop order is an instruction given by you to your bank to pay a creditor.

Chapter Five

LESSON 5

HANDLING DEBT COLLECTORS

In the previous chapter, we spoke about arrears and some important things that you should know how about handling bad debts. We also mentioned the debt collectors you would have to deal with in the event of having accumulated bad debt.

While most of the debt collectors I know are very professional and polite, there are some out there in the industry who can be mean, unfair, opportunistic, and untruthful for their own personal gain. Even though there may be a few of these unprofessional debt collectors out there, I must note that the institutions for which I have worked, where I was actively involved in the day to day business of collecting debts, have never promoted unfair treatment or condoned breaking any laws governing debt collection.

PROFESSIONAL DEBT COLLECTORS

When you are in arrears, you need to engage with a debt collector to make an arrangement to clear the arrears so that the account can be regarded as rehabilitated and no longer a bad debt account.

The debt collector's duty is to act in a professional manner with humanity, but above all they should follow the rules as set out in the

National Debt collection Act 114 of 1998, which regulates the process of collecting debts in South Africa.

A debt collector may work directly for the institution to which the debt is owed or might work for a debt collection agency. A debt collection agency is a company which acts on behalf of a creditor to whom a debt is owed by a person in arrears. Either way, all debt collectors are expected to follow the National Debt collection Act 114 of 1998.

Summary of the National Debt collection Act 114 of 1998

The dos and don'ts of a debt collector:

A debt collector may not use force or threaten to use force against a debtor or any person who has ties with the debtor.

- I have heard sad stories from people where debt collectors took advantage of the situation and threatened either a debtor or a person with whom the debtor had ties. In these situations, the debt collectors were often desperate to collect money and would make such threats in order to manipulate people to make payment. As an example: the debt collector would speak to the debtor and threaten harm against the debtor if payment wasn't made or against a relative of the debtor if they didn't help the debtor to pay the debt.

A debt collector should not be intimidating towards a debtor, or any other person who has ties with the debtor.

- For example, if a debt collector acts in an abusive or overly threatening manner towards a debtor, or a family member of a debtor, in order to secure a payment arrangement. There are some desperate and opportunistic debt collectors who might pull this trick in order to earn their commissions.

Fraudulent and/or misleading representations by debt collectors are prohibited, including actions such as using fraudulent official documents.

- These could be actions such as presenting false information, by means of fraudulent court documents, that give authority to a debt collector (or a representative) to gain access to property in order to attach the goods of a debtor due to non-payment.

A debt collector may not represent him or herself as a police officer, Sheriff, officer of the court or any such person of authority.

- When I was new in the field of debt collection, my employers at the time hired a group of us. They began by training us to ensure that we understood all these rules but some of the members of my group took it upon themselves to intimidate debtors by lying to them. They would say that they were phoning from the police station regarding the debt, and that officers were on the way to arrest them due to non-payment of the debt. Employers are obliged under the law to take immediate disciplinary action against such individuals. (This is a good example of a debt collector falsely representing him or herself in order to threaten and intimidate a debtor or a person related to the debtor.)

A person cannot practice as a debt collector if he or she has been convicted of an offence that has an element of violence, dishonesty, extortion or intimidation.

- Honesty and integrity are essential requirements for anyone who wishes to practice within the financial services industry. Debt Collection falls within these parameters.

A debt collector should not spread, or threaten to spread, false information concerning a debtor's creditworthiness.

- Some debt collectors may attempt to make a person feel pressured into paying their debt by threatening to spread information about the debtor's creditworthiness. No matter whether this information is true or false, a consumer's creditworthiness should always be treated with confidentiality.

A debt collector should never violate the provisions of the code of conduct which stipulates that:

- A person who engages in an act of debt collection on behalf of another person or entity must be registered with the debt collectors council and the company or close corporation that does debt collection must have every director/member registered as well;

- An institution which collects debts without being registered is, by doing so, violating the code of conduct and will be liable for a fine or imprisonment of up to three years. In such an instance, the code of conduct deems any agreements invalid which were entered into between the debt collector and the client (i.e. the creditor/person to whom money is owed), however it doesn't seem to invalidate any agreements made between an unregistered debt collector and the person from whom he/she is collecting;

- If a debt collector harasses you unreasonably, you have the right to ask the debt collector for a copy of his/her registration certificate to prove that he/she is appropriately registered. In the case where a debt collector is not registered in terms of the Debt Collectors Act, he or she is committing an offense which may lead to a penalty;

- Debt collectors are not allowed to contact customers on a Sunday or anytime between 9 pm and 6am. The Debt Collectors Council may take disciplinary action against the debt collector for contacting a debtor between the above prohibited times;

- The code of conduct also prohibits threats made by debt collectors for legal action to follow non-payment if there is no intention to carry out that threat and if there is no instruction to follow up on that threat if the payment is not made. If the debt collector phones repetitively to make such threats, it simply shows that the debt collector doesn't have the mandate or intention to take further legal action. This may be reported to the Debt Collectors Council;

- Under "listing of clients for bad debts", the conduct further stipulates that the debtor may be listed on any credit bureau, provided that the credit provider sent a notice to the debtor advising that they will be listed if he or she doesn't pay within a period of 28 business days as per the provisions of the national credit act. The notice to list a client should also contain warnings to the debtor/client that allow them as a client to understand and exercise other options which are compliant with the law. If a notice is not sent to a client, which serves as a warning or the relevant period for the notice has not elapsed, the listing in the credit bureau is unlawful;

- The conduct also limits the listing of any debt that is unpaid only to debts that fall under the gambit of "credit agreements", as stipulated in the National Credit Act;

- A Debt collector should never phone or contact a customer in relation to a debt that is paid and of which the consumer has furnished the debt collector with the proof that the debt is paid. If the debt collector does this, it will be considered as harassment;

- It is considered an act of extortion by the debt collector should he/she pressure a client to pay or acknowledge a debt which the customer in the normal course of events would never have paid or acknowledged as debt;

- In some instances, the code of conduct states that it is unlawful for a debt collector to insist that the consumer make a payment for amounts that have prescribed. "A prescribed debt can be explained as old debt that has not been acknowledged over a period of three years." *Note that not all debts prescribe within three years. Later in the chapter, we will explore this.

- The code of conduct stipulates that even though there are fees to be charged by debt collectors, the amount which may be charged is limited. In order to make sure that the debt collector bills you the correct amount, in relation to the debt on which they are collecting, you may verify the charges and ensure that they are set to the limits as per those set out in the National Debts Collections Act 114 of 1998. *Note that sometimes mistakes can happen, such as typing errors or system errors which may lead to your account being billed fees which are outside of the limit.

UNPROFFESSIONAL, OPPORTUNISTIC & UNTRUTHFUL DEBT COLLECTORS

These are Debt Collectors who do not follow the code of conduct and the rules set by the National Debt Collectors Act 114 of 1998.

Below are some of the signs that the Debt Collector you are dealing with may be acting unprofessionally:-

- Charging unreasonable fees on the account and also not being transparent about the fees that are charged.

- As a customer, you have a right to be furnished with a full breakdown of all the fees that accumulate on your account. Should the debt collector refuse to provide and/or explain the breakdown of fees, it might be an indication that the Debt Collector may not be acting in good faith.

- They might appear dodgy when requested to share their company details.

- If a debt collector is unwilling to provide details of the institution for which he/she works and/or details about their superiors there may be reason to suspect dishonesty.

OTHER RELEVANT RULES

- **Prescribed debts**

Under the provision of the National Credit Act (NCA), it is stated that the debt is deemed prescribed if the account is dormant (and there is no summons issued or Judgment taken for the debt) for a period of three years or more, the creditor may therefore no longer collect on this debt. However, if any payments are made or the debt is acknowledged then prescription may be interrupted and collection may proceed.

Note that not all debts prescribe within three years. Below is a list of the debts which only prescribe in thirty years:-

- Home loans

- Taxes owed to SARS

- TV Licences

- Municipal accounts

- **The in duplum rule**

This rule regulates the interest charged on an account. Basically, it prohibits creditors from running interest on an account once the interest charged has accrued to an amount equal to the outstanding principal debt.

An example of this would be a scenario where an amount of R5 000.00 is borrowed and, over time, an interest amount of R5 000.00 is accumulated on the account making up a total of R10 000.00. The creditor is obligated to stop any further interest from accumulating on the account once that stage is reached.

These are some of the things that you can check and calculate to make sure that you are paying only for what you are legally liable.

Chapter Six

LESSON 6

SELLING OR BUYING A HOUSE

To those that are in the process of buying property in these times, I would like to congratulate you and wish you the best of luck going forward. To those who are still planning to buy, I'd like to take this opportunity to share with you how you can make sure that you get the best value for your money when buying a property.

In my time working for a bank, my biggest exposure (in terms of the products sold by a bank) is the home loan product. I have accumulated much information that could help you when buying a property and even some knowledge that could be useful should you face a time when you would need to surrender ownership of your property. Buying a property is a huge achievement and brings so much satisfaction, especially in a tough economy such as the one in which we are currently living. Conversely, it may be entirely the opposite of that sense of joy and achievement, when being put in a position of having to sell a property.

SELLING A HOUSE IN TOUGH TIMES

In a tough economy, many people find themselves having to sell their houses, whether voluntarily or involuntarily. The best option would be to try to sell the house voluntarily.

VOLUNTARY SALE

Private sales are a type of voluntary sale which are initiated by the owner of the property, with or without the intervention of an estate agent. Usually a property owner approaches a bank, or an estate agent, or even advertises a property via other channels to get a prospective buyer.

There are many advantages to selling a property privately, rather than being in a situation where the mortgager/financier of your property initiates a forced sale on your property via the foreclosure route. One advantage is saving on additional costs, as legal fees will be incurred the moment a financier initiates the foreclosure process and these will be added onto the outstanding balance of the defaulter's loan.

Below are some tips for selling your property privately:

- You can market your property on any public channel that permits advertising: utilise social media, or your friends (via word of mouth), as a selling tool. You may be lucky, and find a buyer.
- By opting to find a buyer on your own, you can avoid paying estate agent fees and by using social media, you can avoid marketing costs.

An Estate agent's fee is usually a percentage of the total amount offered by the buyer and accepted by the seller. For example, a 6% agents' fee on a selling price of R1 000 000.00, means that the estate agent will be entitled to R60 000.00 of the R1 000 000.00 Having to pay this fee gets even harder if you are in a position where you are forced to sell a house that is situated in an area where there is less demand for property. In such a situation, you may be compelled to accept an offer that is less than what you owe the bank. For example, you may still owe R1 200 000.00 on your bond but only receive an offer for R1 000 000.00. Having to deduct the 6% which is due to the estate agent will then just further reduce the amount that can be paid off on your existing home loan, and this is before calculating any of the other expenses incurred when selling a house (other expenses which we will look at later). Thus, selling a house direct, without involving an estate agent, can save you a lot of money you cannot afford to lose.

When I released my first book titled, "Automotive Excellence", I did a lot of marketing online, even on social media. With social media, you can set up adverts tailored to your specific criteria. I'll just use one channel as an example here and then it will be up to you to explore and make use of the many other available channels online.

So let's look at Facebook. First of all, you create a profile page, and then you can post information and images of the items that you are selling. When posting on your page, you will be given the option to play around with your target market as Facebook allows you to specify who exactly you want to target. For example, your target market may be selected via different variables such as age, interests and demographics.

Let's explore the selection of these variables though a practical example in the case study below.

CASE STUDY:

You are a married couple, living in Johannesburg South, who is expecting your first baby. You are currently living in a one-bedroom apartment, which you bought five years back when you got married, but now that you are expecting a baby you want to move to a bigger house where you would have a separate bedroom for the child.

Your task now, is to find someone suitable who would appreciate your current living conditions. So as a first step you go to Facebook, (which has various options to promote your advert through its model of finding a suitable match) to advertise your house.

One of the variables required for the target audience for your advert, is that you will be asked to specify the age group you wish to target. This will help you to narrow down your audience to the people that are more likely to be interested in the property you are selling e.g. young singles or newly married couples with no children. Going further, it will ask you to specify demographics, namely the general area in which your target audience is situated e.g. Gauteng (it is rare for people outside of your general area to buy property in your area). As you continue you will need, or be required, to provide various general answers, like what other qualities your target market should have, in order to focus on the most likely candidates. Now this is one of the bigger advantages because social media can identify and target a person who is interested in property, such as a potential property investor or an individual who is interested in buying a residential home.

As an alternative to social media, you could approach your property financiers to find out if they could offer any assistance with selling your property. Most financial institutions are willing to offer some help.

Selling a house, especially a home where you've made lots of special memories, may trigger many different emotions. Just imagine having to sell a house you moved into on your wedding day, even if the motivation to sell came from starting a family. Reasons such as these cause one to become very sentimental about a house and sometimes make it more difficult to let it go. Now imagine having to sell that property because you cannot afford it anymore.

In times like these, your decision making is likely to be compromised by emotion. Making the situation worse, is that you may be in the desperate situation of having to accept an offer on your property that will leave you with a shortfall on your mortgage loan and this might also negatively impact your credit record. Even once your bond has been cancelled and the property is no longer in your name, the outstanding balance continues to be reported on the credit bureaus for as long as there is still money owed to the lender on your mortgage loan. In many cases, I've seen people struggling to pay this residual debt for years after the house is sold.

Property values, and therefore selling prices, are generally dictated by demand in the market and in your area, so making your house as attractive as possible and without defect, may assist you to obtain a viable offer when selling your house.

Below are a few ideas to make your property more appealing:

- Your house should be in a condition that would make a prospective buyer not only feel comfortable, but also excited by the idea of buying it. Although having shelter is a basic need, people don't consider buying a house just as a shelter over their heads. So adding a few cosmetic improvements here and there can help get you closer to negotiating a better offer. Things that make the house look neat, such as tiles or wooden flooring in the bedrooms rather than carpets. (Many people nowadays prefer not to sleep in bedrooms with carpets due to health reasons such as sinusitis).

- Doing renovations and making improvements are good ways to increase the value of your investment, or to maximize your nett proceeds when selling your property, even though it might be difficult when you are caught up in a tight financial position. Should you consider making structural changes or additions to your property, it is important however, to take building legislation into consideration before proceeding with anything. If any alterations or improvements are made without an approved building plan, you may get fined or even prosecuted and then end up having to demolish all the illegal additions, thereby putting you in an even worse financial position. When a property is placed on the market for sale, part of the procedure is that a full valuation is conducted to establish the value of the property and to ensure that any defects and improvements are noted. Now in cases where there are illegal alterations, they are not taken into consideration on the valuation and they don't increase the value of the property.

- Upgrading the Security of your property is another way to influence the selling price of your home. It is not only beneficial when selling your home, but also while you are still living there. However, I think it is good to know when to stop when it comes to tightening your security; meaning that you should not make unnecessary upgrades. Too much security can be a red flag for a prospective buyer, as it may be an indicator that your property is in high crime zone. I personally look for these red flags when searching for a new home, so if I notice that the seller has applied too much security, I usually assume that the area has too much crime.

- Make use of any extra space such as a huge garage. Some people convert unused garages into flats or create a living space above the garage. This comes in handy as extra storage space or can be rented out as a living space to make some extra income. This is often a good selling point when marketing the property as the prospective buyer may need the additional income, or he may like the idea of the additional income offered by renting out the space.

- Having additional storage space can increase the demand for your house and benefit you while you are staying in the house. No matter how large or small your home is, there are always things that need to be stored away, either for future use or just for sentimental reasons. I'm one of those people who loves to store away things that I've received as gifts from loved ones, ranging from wine bottles, dishes and glasses to old clothes and toys. Fortunately having extra closet space around my house fulfils this need for me, but storage space for a larger family would be more challenging. Sufficient or surplus storage is always a 'cherry on top' and highly valued when people are looking to buy a new property.

- Keep ceilings and roofs well maintained as a dirty or stained ceiling could indicate that the roof is leaking and needs to be repaired. It can be very costly to fix a roof so this will discourage prospective buyers.

- Going green can help you save money on electricity bills. Going green or living green means that you are making environmentally friendly decisions. The tenets of going green are, "Reduce, Re-use and Recycle," which are the practices of a responsible lifestyle that protects the environment and helps to sustain its natural resources. Informing a prospective buyer that you have installed devices such as geyser timers, or timers for pool pumps and fountains, may be the added benefits that encourage prospective buyers to make a good offer on your property.

- Environmental safety within the home is always an important consideration. Prior to placing your property on the market, it is good practice to assess whether your house has all the necessary safety features in place to attract a prospective buyer. For example, if your staircase doesn't have railings, it could appear unsafe to many people who are afraid to climb stairs without holding on to something. Exposed electrical wiring may also be a red flag indicating a lack of safety or environmental friendliness, especially if the buyer has children or pets. Safety, security and environmental friendliness might be very important to the prospective buyer, but may be unaffordable to him as an added cost, so it is vital to ensure that it is already in place. Keep in mind that, although there are people who buy houses with the purpose of fixing them up and then re-selling, most buyers' buying power is likely to be exhausted after the purchase of the house and they may be discouraged should there be too many things to fix. Alternatively, upgrades and good maintenance will encourage people to buy.

EXPENSES INCURRED WHEN SELLING A HOUSE

One of the reasons I touched on ideas to maximise your selling price is because there are some, mostly unavoidable, expenses attached to selling a house.

Below is a list of expenses typically incurred when selling a property:

It is important to note that the amounts presented below are estimates only and do not reflect actual costs; for example, estate agents commission will not always be 6%. The template lists the various types of expense which may be incurred during the cancellation process when a transfer of ownership takes place. This may be used as a guideline to budget for the expenses that you will incur when selling a house as it will assist you to anticipate what your profit or loss might be in the event your property is sold successfully.

FEE TEMPLATE	COSTS
SELLING PRICE -	R 950 000.00
LESS 6% AGENTS COMM -	R 57 000
CANCELLATION COST -	R 2 000.00
RATES & TAXES -	R 3 500.00
REPAIRS -	R 0.00
LEGAL FEES -	R 0.00
LEVIES -	R 0.00
UPLIFTMENT OF INTERDICT-	R 800.00
ECC / BEETLE CERT / PLUMMING CERT-	R 500.00
BRIDGING FINANCE INTEREST-	R 0.00
+ OCCUPATION RENT -	R 0.00
THIRD PARTY INTERDICT -	R 0.00
NETT PROCEEDS -	R 886 200.00

Further explanation of each expense:

Selling Price

Selling price is the total amount offered by the buyer to purchase the property.

Now, let's say that you have managed to bump up your selling price. You did a few upgrades and managed to get a buyer to sign an offer to purchase, either through an estate agent or privately. You now need to calculate whether you are likely to make a profit or a loss from the sale.

Estate Agents' Commission

In the event that you utilise the services of an estate agent to find a buyer for your property, you will agree on a fee (usually a percentage of the selling price) which will be deducted from the purchase price once the property is registered in the buyers' name, unless you agree to pay the agent separately. Note that there is usually no fee payable should the agent be unsuccessful in finding a buyer. In most cases a contract will be signed with an agent. This allows him/her a sole mandate to market your property for a period of time. In cases where a property is difficult to sell, or needs to be sold quickly, the mandate may be shared by two or more agents but the full agreed fee will be paid to the successful agent. However, as I mentioned previously, in order to maximise your profit or mitigate your loss, you may elect to market your property on your own and once you have an interested buyer you can buy an offer to purchase contract from stores like CNA. Always be careful of possible scams. Never include too many personal details upfront that might provide loopholes for scammers and fraudsters. If you make use of an estate agent, make sure that you read and fully understand the contents of the contract before you sign anything, especially details relating to termination of the contract. In instances where a sole mandate is granted, the exposure which your property receives will be limited to a single agent for a specified period.

Cancellation costs

It is required by law that this fee is paid in order to terminate a seller's ownership of a property. The deed registered in the seller's name must be cancelled so that the deeds office can prepare for a bond to be registered in the name of the new owner. Note that you would only be paying for the cost of the cancellation; registration costs are paid by the new owner.

Rates and Taxes

If there are any outstanding rates and taxes owed to the municipality, you will need to settle those fees before the sale can proceed. It's always best to make sure that you pay these fees regularly every month as payment of these fees in full are non-negotiable in order to transfer ownership of a property. If there are fees outstanding, it may delay the cancellation process as the municipality, or city council, will not issue a clearance certificate until all payments are up to date. A clearance certificate has to be given with all the other required documents to the Deeds office for registration. The longer transfer is delayed, the more money you are likely to lose due to monthly interest and service fees on your existing mortgage loan, among others.

Outstanding levies

As with rates and taxes on a free standing property, levies have to be up to date in order for a clearance certificate to be issued. This applies to any property which is part of a Sectional Title development.

Repairs

Should the property need any repairs before the buyer takes transfer, the parties can negotiate whether the repairs are to be completed at the cost of the seller prior to registration, or alternatively that the cost be deducted from the purchase price and this will then also negatively affect the nett proceeds amount.

Legal Fees

If any legal action has been taken against you by your mortgagor there could be various legal fees that need to be paid prior to transfer. Most of these fees are paid from your mortgage loan account upon completion of the action by the appointed litigation attorney but if an interdict has been placed on your property, it will have to be uplifted before transfer can take place. The cost of uplifting the interdict will be deducted from the purchase price. Note that an interdict is placed on a property by a creditor as part of the legal process, in the form of an attachment order, so that a property may be sold at a sale in execution. As this interdict is noted at the deeds office it has to be removed, with the consent of the bondholder, before a transfer can take place. It is important to know also, that an interdict may be placed on a property by a third party i.e. any other person or institution to whom you are indebted and where there have been defaults on payment. These third party interdicts can often delay a transfer for months, as they are usually only discovered at the point of registration when documents have been sent for approval by the registrar of deeds. Only then can the attorney trace the relevant creditor to obtain permission for the upliftment to be done.

Electrical compliance certificate

An Electrical Compliance Certificate, or ECC, is a certificate that certifies that the electrical installations in the house are compliant with the requirements that are specified in the Occupational Health and Safety Act. This certificate has to be obtained before the transfer can take place.

Beetle Certificate

This is a certificate issued to confirm that any accessible wood, which makes up the whole or part of the permanent structure of the property is not contaminated by insects that are likely to destroy or weaken these structures. These certificates are valid for a period of two years and can therefore be reused for any transfer taking place within that time.

Plumbing certificate

This is to certify that all the plumbing in the relevant property complies with the regulatory installation requirements.

Occupational rent

In some instances a buyer wishes, or is willing, to occupy the property before the transfer takes place. It's a good thing for the buyer in that it gives him/her time to pick up any hidden faults or issues on the property that might need attention. The buyer will therefore be liable for occupational rent from date of occupation to date of registration and this will reflect as a credit on the invoice. Occupational rent is usually charged at 1% of the purchase price over the agreed period.

Anticipated interest

The transfer process takes about three months as long as there are no complications or delays, so it is wise to take into consideration the interest that will accumulate on your mortgage loan balance and include it in your expense calculations. To be safe, confirm the estimated amount with your bondholder.

Nett proceeds

Once all the identified expenses are subtracted from, and any occupational rental added to, the purchase price, you will arrive at the figure that will be paid to settle your bond and thus be able to calculate the profit or loss that you will take from the transaction.

Involuntary Sale

An involuntary sale, or sale in execution, is when your house is placed on auction by your credit provider and sold by the Sheriff of the court, usually because you have defaulted on your loan repayments for several months. In most instances, this drastic action is taken as a last resort by creditors in order to recover the debt owed to them.

This process begins once a debtor has defaulted on his/her payments for around three months and has failed to contact the creditor to make a payment arrangement to catch up on his/her arrears. As mentioned briefly in a previous chapter, the first step in the legal process is a letter of demand (now called a section 129 letter under the National Credit Act). The second step is a Summons (Foreclosure Notice) which is authorised by the court and delivered by the Sheriff. The third step is either a Default (undefended) or Summary (defended) Judgement (this is where you become blacklisted). This order is also granted by the court and gives the creditor the right to proceed to the fourth step which is the Writ of Attachment, also authorised by the court and personally delivered by the Sheriff. Once this notice has been delivered, an interdict is placed on the property in the deeds office and the creditor is permitted to proceed with a sale in execution. A notice of sale is placed in a local newspaper and the Government Gazette, and is then auctioned by the Sheriff of the court at his offices, or more rarely, at the property.

The biggest problem with this option, apart from being blacklisted, is that a property sold in this way is usually sold at a loss. Whether it is bought by a third party, or bought by the creditor, the purchase price is unlikely to cover your full debt and you will still be liable to pay off the shortfall, plus interest.

Your best option is to be prepared. Always be aware of your financial situation and don't be too proud to ask your creditor for assistance as soon as you find yourself in trouble. They can also assist and advise you with regards to selling your property before you find yourself in a situation as discussed above. Where possible, make sure that your property is always well maintained and in a good condition.

BUYING A PROPERTY

We will not dwell much on the topic of buying a property as this book is more concerned with equipping you to survive tough times, but I would like to discuss a few concerns with regards to buying a property, which might affect you negatively.

PREPARE YOURSELF TO OWN A HOME

Buying a home, if you don't have cash, requires that you obtain finance in the form of a mortgage loan. Being successful in obtaining a bond will require that you have a credit score that is good enough for a creditor to consider your application.

Below are some tips that may help you when buying a house:

- Start by identifying what your requirements are.

Do you want a permanent residence or holiday home for your own exclusive use, or are you looking to buy a property as an investment to fix up and re-sell or rent out? Either way, do your homework regarding the area you wish to buy in, with regards to crime, proximity to schools, travel routes, and shopping centres etc. Also look at demand in the area which will affect your resale value, especially if you are looking to try and sell in the short term. If you want a property to rent out, make sure you buy in an area with high demand for rentals.

- Check your credit score to see if you are likely to qualify for a home loan.

The better your score is, the cheaper your interest rate is likely to be. Also let me tell you something that most people don't know about interest rates; they can be reviewed. At any stage after you get your bond approved, as long as you have been making regular payments, you can call your credit provider and ask for your interest rate to be reviewed. If your credit score and profile is good and you meet the terms and conditions, they might consider reducing your interest rate: note that interest rates are related to risk, so the less risk you pose to a credit provider, the more likely he is to grant you a lower interest rate.

- Decide if you will be buying alone or with a partner.

Buying a home with a partner means that you both need to be in good standing with your credit profiles, as the creditor will do credit checks on both of you once a joint application is received.

- Decide on the type of house that you want to buy and be aware of additional expenses.

Levies must be paid when you own sectional title properties, such as flats and townhouses, and rates and taxes are payable on free-standing properties (note that these costs vary a lot depending on the complex or the area). Some people forget to factor in these costs when budgeting and focus only on the bond instalment.

- Other considerations when deciding between a free-standing property and a sectional title.

With a free-standing property you will have a lot more freedom to decide on cosmetics such as paint colours and structural additions or changes. Most complexes prefer uniformity and are unlikely to agree to any changes you may wish to make, especially on the outside.

- Building loans.

An important thing to be aware of with this type of loan is that repayments to the creditor start as soon as funds are paid out to the contractor, not once the property is complete and the full loan has been released. The creditor will release funds as required by the builder (known as progress payments) and requires repayment from you as soon as the first amounts are paid out. (Your loan term begins and interest accumulates from this date.)

- Pay attention to the terms and conditions on the offer to purchase.

These can sometimes be tricky and you need to ensure that you are fully cognisant of all the terms you agree to before you sign the document. Be aware that you are allowed a cooling off period should you wish to retract your offer, and make sure that you know when it ends. If you cancel your offer after this period, you may be liable to pay penalties to both the seller and the agent for wasted costs and/or loss of income.

There are many factors to consider before buying or selling a house and this chapter should give you some idea of how to prepare. The most important thing, especially when entering into any major financial contract, is to be aware of all your options.

Chapter Seven

LESSON 7

THE FUTURE OF TRANSACTING AND BANKING THE DIGITAL SOLUTIONS

WHAT IS THE FUTURE OF BANKING?

Change is the only thing that is constant in this world.

Look how the world has evolved around messaging. We started by sending messages via notes, fast mail, letters, faxes, emails and so on. Now we have phones and cool apps which we can use to message each other instantly, without the hassle of having to depend on people at a post office to deliver our letters, or worry that the paper in our fax machines may run out at any time. It's important to know the future, or at least try to predict it, as you are then more likely to be prepared to deal with the changes when they reach you.

The best way to deal with change is to embrace it.

Look at how the world is evolving around payments. In ancient times people used to barter and exchange items, sometimes without considering or understanding, the fair value of the bartered items before engaging in a transaction. Payment methods have evolved from exchanging a cow for gold, to exchanging a cow for money and from exchanging land for a mirror, to exchanging a mirror for small change.

Thanks to this evolution, we can be more confident in receiving value in exchange for our money, as many older methods of transaction were not fair! One party usually lost, while the other gained a lot more than they should have. This is why the banking world is constantly evolving and changing to make transacting easier and more effective.

ONE OF THE MORE RECENT CHANGES TO PROMOTE FAIRNESS IS THE DEBICHECK

A new form of debit order payment, called the DebiCheck, is emerging. It works a little differently from the traditional way of capturing, approving and processing debit orders. This method is stricter and is aimed at eliminating debit order abuse by both the customer and the institution which processes the debit order.

Definition

DebiCheck is a type of debit order that you confirm via your electronic device at inception of your contract. This gives the bank the assurance that there is a mandate between the consumer and the institution processing the debit order.

A SUMMARY OF THE FACTS

Why the introduction of DebiCheck?

Debit orders have been overly abused in the past, both by the consumer and the institution processing the debit orders on the accounts of consumers. Consumers have been disputing and reversing debit orders, most often because they are struggling to manage their daily finances as per the findings of the Payments Association of South Africa (PASA).

The South African Reserve Bank (SARB) became concerned and decided to intervene in this issue, with the assistance of PASA.

As for PASA, their long-term goal is to eventually have all companies on this system, meaning that in the near future any and all companies that process debit orders have to utilise this method. I can imagine that it will result in far better control over, and prevent manipulation of, the use of debit orders by customers and institutions.

As for consumers, once an agreement for an institution to deduct funds has been entered into, consumers are required to confirm the details of the debit order on an electronic device such as an ATM, a banking App, or on a website that belongs to their bank.

Additionally, as part of the process, the bank will require further verification where you have to confirm your action in agreeing to the mandate. For example, when you pay a recipient from your online banking, the banks will SMS an OTP number to your cell phone so that you can verify the transaction. This gives them further confirmation that it is the correct person who loaded the transaction or gave them authority to distribute funds from an account.

Confirmation will only occur once, at the beginning of the contract, unless there are changes to the debit order details - changes such as the amount being debited.

As a consumer, what is most important to know is that all your debit orders must be mandated, even the ones that were processed on your account prior to the introduction of DebiCheck. By mandated, I simply mean the action of being authorised by you as a consumer, either by telephone or via a written instruction.

For more information on this, you can check the PASA website: www.pasa.org.za

FINDING YOUR DIGITAL SOLUTION

It's important to understand exactly what you want to do, so that if you don't know a specific digital way of doing it, you can phone your bank to ask them to explain the process to you. I can assure you that the vast majority of the things that you can do in the branch are possible to do on your phone, tablet or pc.

Ask and you shall receive, and you will surely find your solution. You don't always need to have all the answers, just learn to ask for help when you need it.

My lesson in this is that there is always the option to call your bank for assistance if you are unsure about a process or shortcut.

I needed a shortcut one day. I was in traffic, nowhere near a branch and evening was approaching. This meant that any chance I had to get to a branch, would still have meant that I arrived too late to get any service. The best option to find my solution was to phone my bank to request assistance in finding the way forward.

Whether it's a transaction or any other bank related query, times have changed. All the help you need is at your fingertips.

SOME OF THE TRANSACTIONS THAT YOU CAN DO FROM YOUR PHONE

BY USSD –

- Withdraw cash without a bank card. There may be times when you forget your bank card at home
- Make once-off payments (transfer money to someone else's bank account)
- Check your bank balances
- Make cell-phone payments (payment to a phone number)
- Reverse cell-phone payments
- Process a loan application
- Open a savings account
- Open an investment account
- Get Insurance

- Get a cell-phone contract
- Buy airtime

WHAT IS USSD?

It's an acronym which stands for Unstructured Supplementary Service Data. It's been around for some time now, and I'm sure at some point you noticed instances where you were able to communicate with a service provider or institution by dialling a number that looks something like: *0*00*0000#. (Note this is not an actual number used to obtain service, but merely an example of the format.) The pattern of numbers that you use to buy airtime or submit your name for a competition operates under the USSD function.

BY ONLINE BANKING –

- Purchase pre-paid airtime
- Purchase pre-paid electricity
- Manage your credit or cheque card
- Increase or decrease limits for those cards
- Add benefits for your regular payments

BY SELF-HELP BANKING –

You need to be intricately familiar with digital banking to be fully proficient in helping yourself, or in serving all your own banking needs.

Imagine how easy things would be if you could be your own clothing designer, medical doctor, lawyer and financial advisor?

Give power to the client, and enable the client to keep more money for himself!

That's how we perceive self-help at the bank.

This would mean that you wouldn't have to distribute as much of your hard-earned cash. Because you could handle your own divorce case, design your own clothes, and consult yourself in medical or financial situations you would save a lot of money by being able to do almost everything for yourself.

The concept of self-help banking is structured somewhat like the above scenario, whereby you are equipped to do the majority of banking processes by yourself; things that you would usually have to pay another person to do for you.

Because financial institutions are constantly competing amongst one another for business, the focus is on you. Financial institutions are fighting for the privilege of enabling you to achieve your goals. The best way they have found to do this, is to encourage you to empower yourself by being as independent from the bank as possible (with the added incentive of saving money you might otherwise have spent on services) so that they have more time to spend on further innovations to make your banking life easier. This is the intention of self-help banking.

TECHNOLOGY IS THE NEW OXYGEN

These days, we have complex devices that we refer to as smart phones. They might be complex in terms of defining what they do and how they do it, but in the end they fulfil the purpose of enabling us to survive and breathe freely. Technology is the new oxygen we breathe! For our purposes, it's not important to explain the process that enables us to breathe; the only thing that I would like to point out about breathing is that it is the act of drawing air through my lungs which enables me to survive and enjoy each day. In the same way, the use of technology in your day-to-day banking activities allows you to function as an entity within the economy.

AND MORE IS COMING...

A while back I was invited to attend an event by an independent company: an event outside of my work which had nothing to do with the company that I work for. This company informed us about a new technological advancement on which they are working. It's technology that will do away with the need to carry multiple cards in our wallets. Basically, as time goes by and financial institutions continue to form more alliances with retailers, garages and other businesses, there will come a time when people will be able to carry a single card which will allow them to transact with all retailers and financial institutions. For example,; currently the average person might carry a debit card, credit card, a few clothing store cards and a variety of cards that earn savings points. This company informed us that they intend to merge all these cards into one universal card.

There are more exciting things coming, but it remains important to ensure that you don't fall victim to scams. So, let us move on to the next chapter which has crucial information about what you need to do to protect yourself from thieves who are always on the lookout for fresh victims.

Chapter Eight

LESSON 8

PHISHING AND FRAUD

DEFINITION OF PHISHING

Phishing is the term used to describe the act of criminal entities trying to obtain sensitive personal information from their targets. These people will try to get you to freely give them information like passwords, ID numbers, bank account details and pin numbers by sending out emails or text messages that look legitimate. The methods they use, whether they phone, email, text, or even fax you, will make the communication seem as valid and authentic as if it came from a trusted institution.

How can you identify a scam?

Without exception, these types of messages from scammers will require that you give out confidential information. If you think about it logically, you would realise that your bank already has all the information about you that they need; they would not have allowed you to open a bank account without having your ID number, date of birth and salary details. Am I making sense? Also, when you open a banking account you will receive a bank card with a pin number, hence the bank will always have a record of your card number and pin codes.

Another tell-tale sign that someone is phishing is that they are unlikely to address you by name, but will start a communication by addressing you as, "Dear valued customer".

Fraudsters are constantly inventing new ways to fleece people, so there are always cases being reported, even though security technology is continually improving and evolving to keep up.

In April 2018, SAFPS (South African Fraud Prevention Service) issued a press release about the concerning issue of the growing fraud statistics and in 2020 the statistics keep rising due to increased reliance on technology during the Covid-19 pandemic.

FRAUD AND PAYMENT SCAMS

The story of my Zimbabwean friend

I've always been blessed by being able to learn from other people's mistakes. When a former neighbour of mine found himself in a situation where he was unable to make rational decisions regarding a new employment offer, he was forced to make sacrifices, some of which were too painful and uncomfortable to discuss here. But basically, because of the desperate situation that he was in, he let himself be deceived by fraudsters. These cybercriminals took advantage of him; simply by gathering information they somehow managed to determine that he was in a desperate situation.

Due to technological advances and convenience, online payments are becoming increasingly popular; even social media platforms are embracing the convenience of online payments these days. More and more retail industries are embracing the culture of showcasing their goods and services and reaching their target markets online, in order to conclude successful sales transactions. Then there is also the fact that people are getting more comfortable with the convenience of buying what they need, without the struggle of waiting in line at checkout counters.

The sad part is that fraudsters have adopted a similar pattern to the retail industries. They showcase their non-existent goods and services to reach the people who fall for their tricks, and then milk their money out of them.

My friend, who had to leave South Africa to go back to Zimbabwe, was desperate to sell his furniture prior to his departure, so he used the internet to advertise and soon received a phone call from a guy who seemed interested in buying everything.

Desperation attracts fraudsters to you! It's like honey to a bee for fraudsters and phishers.

This guy promised to do an EFT (electronic funds transfer) as payment for the items. An hour after concluding his conversation with this buyer, my friend got an SMS notification, as well as an email confirmation, affirming that he had received the agreed payment amount from another bank. (Due to his desperation to sell the furniture, my friend was not alerted by the fact that the purchaser never requested his address to view the furniture before making the payment.) Later the same day, my friend received another call from the buyer (phisher) asking whether he had received the funds and then asked my friend for the address where he could collect the furniture. Believing everything was in order, my friend provided the address and the buyer (phisher) collected the furniture.

The following day my friend checked his account expecting the funds to reflect, but they never did. That is when things started to go sour. He phoned his bank, who told him to call the bank from where the funds were transferred (as per the proof of the fake SMS and e-mail that the buyer provided to lure him into believing that that the transaction actually occurred) and they in turn asked him to provide the reference number of the transaction from the proof of payment he received via e-mail. When he provided the reference number, the bank advised that the reference number didn't exist.

He had been scammed! There was never any payment made to his account.

You see, he had been so desperate to get rid of his things and receive payment that he neglected to verify the details sent to him before letting his furniture go.

A story from when I owned a small business

In 2014, while I was running a small catering business, I received a call from a potential client who wanted me to email him a quotation for my services. The amount I quoted, for what he required, came to a total of R9, 600.00.

Soon after sending the quotation, I received a bank notification stating that R19, 600.00 had been paid to my bank account. Then, a few minutes later, the client called again and said he had transferred R19, 600.00 by mistake and asked that I refund the difference of R10, 000.00 to him. He further requested that I e-wallet at least R3, 000.00 to his cell number as he needed it urgently, but said that he was willing to wait for the rest.

I immediately called my bank to enquire about the transaction and they told me that a cheque had been deposited, but advised me to wait for at least seven days for the funds to reflect in my account. They further advised that I should not refund anything to the client, before the cheque cleared, especially if I was not 100% certain of its validity. Seven days passed and I received a notification from my bank stating that the cheque was unpaid. The cheque didn't clear; it was invalid. So, if I had been desperate to secure this client and neglected to verify the validity of the transaction, I would most likely have processed the e-wallet payment to him and lost at least R3, 000.00.

Most of the people who have been defrauded are desperate in some way, and desperation often leads to negligence. Unfortunately, criminal elements are constantly on the lookout for victims who are vulnerable to their attacks and will take advantage of anyone who is not consistently vigilant.

PERSONAL LOAN SCAMS

"Deception may give us what we want for the present, but it will always take it away in the end"

— RACHEL HAWTHORNE

At a point in their lives when things get tough and they need a loan, some people get so desperate that they start to search the internet for any companies that might offer them loans, even if they have a bad credit history.

This is when the personal loan scammers take advantage. On a google search you might find something like, **"Get a personal loan for an amount up to R150 000, with a low interest rate. Blacklisted people are also welcome to apply. Get approved same day, and the money will be deposited to your account the same day"**.

This may sound appealing to someone who has been declined loans from his bank; it sounds so easy and offers relief from a dire situation. But this is how scammers operate. They tell you what you want to hear and they make it look as if they can help you solve all your problems. They offer the bait and once you are hooked, they reveal their true deception.

After you fall for this wonderful proposal from an unknown company, offering you this loan that you have been trying to get for ages so that you can use it to pay your children's school fees, or fix your car, or fulfil any financial goal that requires financing; you give them your details. They will often make the application look legitimate on their website and request that you provide all the information that would normally be asked on loan application-details such as your ID number, bank details (so that you may receive the funds as promised), salary payment date and so forth…

A day goes by, then a week or more but you still receive no contract for the loan, even though you gave them all your details. Soon it's your salary day and you receive payment from your employer; then boom, a new debit order goes through on your account and it's from this company that accepted your loan application. You phone them, but now they tell you a different story; it's no longer about them giving you a loan, it's about them charging you a service fee for helping you find a loan. Many of these dodgy companies do that, they phrase everything in such a way that you believe that you have qualified to receive a loan from them, but you are never advised of their real intentions until it is too late.

For more information about this issue, do a google search on personal loan scams.

SOME TIPS ON HOW TO PROTECT YOURSELF FROM FRAUD AND PHISHING

- As I mentioned before, your bank should already have all your details. They will never ask you to confirm your login details via a link on email or SMS. Some scammers may send you an email to request that you update your login details by clicking on a link provided in their email. That's completely wrong! You cannot update your login details by responding to an email.
- Make sure to update your antivirus application regularly, and most importantly, ensure that you update it from a trusted source.
- Never access your bank accounts from an internet cafe computer.
- Never allow friends or family to utilize your phone, laptop or desktop while you are logged on to your online banking.

- Never access your bank's website through received links. Always go to your browser and type the bank's website to log in. Because when you access via received links, the password that you type in may be sent to criminals who will then easily be able to access your online banking profile. It's easy for fraudsters to deceive you by sending links. For example, let's say that your bank's web address is www.sibonisoBank.com. Fraudsters might send you a link that looks very similar to your bank's website by changing one or two characters, like the following: www.sib0nisobank.co.za. Did you notice the difference between the two? Possibly you did, but it's normal to miss small details sometimes; perhaps when you are tired or trying to get through things fast. The difference between the two is that the original website only contains letters whereas the fake version contains the number 0 instead of the letter o and also changes the capital B to a small b. Should you mistakenly access this website, it will be easy for the fraudsters to obtain your personal information.
- What I've always observed as good practice, is to not use the same password for everything. It's a bad idea to have the same passwords for your banking accounts as for your google accounts, email accounts and login details for home or work computers; who knows, what if the IT guy from work manages to steal your login details?
- Always remember to log out as soon as you are done using your internet banking application or online banking.
- It's wise to change your pins and passwords frequently.
- Never save your sensitive personal information on your computer, especially information such as passwords and pin numbers. Try also not to write them down if you can help it. It's always best to have a password that is personal to you and can be remembered easily so that no-one else can gain access to your applications.

- Try, however, to make sure that it's not a common word or name that your friends or family could easily guess.
- Be realistic about how much you allow yourself to withdraw from an ATM and transfer daily when you set your daily limits. (You can always change your limits for special circumstances when you may require more.) This may help you reduce your losses should a fraudster obtain your details. Remember also, that it is safer to have a card than carry a lot of cash these days. Most businesses have adapted to allowing clients use cards to pay for goods as it is safer than having a lot of cash on the premises.
- Avoid using public Wi-Fi (especially for banking).
- Don't ever store sensitive information about your bank cards, pin codes, internet banking, or internet transaction details onto your mobile devices.
- When you sell a mobile device, or give it away to someone else, please make sure to reset it to the factory default settings. This will ensure that your information, or any data that you have used to access your accounts, will be wiped out before anyone can potentially take advantage of it.
- Most importantly, don't ever act out of desperation because criminals can sense it through your actions. See my stories which illustrate how acting out of desperation can lead to even bigger problems within a short time.
- Avoid sharing too much personal information about yourself on social media. Social media is one of the most useful tools for fraudsters. They can easily keep track of your habits and study you to their own satisfaction.
- I touched on the future of transacting and banking in the previous chapter to illustrate how the simplest and best way to transact will now be via Apps. Many companies, retailers, clothing shops, hardware stores, and even food shops have welcomed the use of Apps for transacting and interacting with customers. It is however, vital for you to be cautious from which source you download these Apps. Ensure that

you only download Apps from trusted sources. Hackers and fraudsters also create fake Apps with the intention of getting your sensitive information. Always ask your service provider or bank about which platforms they recommend for you to download their Apps.

- If possible, find out if the Apps or platforms that you are using are 2FA enabled. A 2FA is a secondary method of assuring that the person logging into the App or system is truly authorised to log on. For example, you log on to a website with your password and over and above the password you entered; the financial service provider will send a notification to your phone to ask you to verify the authorization to log on.

OTHER BLIND SPOTS TO BE WARY OF

Over and above these tips, I personally feel that it is a good idea to add protection of your signature to the measures you use to protect yourself against fraud. You can do this by ensuring that the documents you sign are never exposed to third parties who have no reason to access them.

Never expose your debit card or credit card details to people, or leave your cards lying around carelessly, because some online payments are easily processed by entering your card details. Fraudsters might take pictures of your card and in so doing, will be able to process payments online by using the snapshots of your card details. All they need is the card number, expiry date, card holder name and CVC (security verification code), which is the number at the back of your card. Yes, it's as simple as that. I'm not trying to give anyone ideas of how to commit criminal offenses, just alerting people on how to protect their information.

HOW ARTIFICIAL INTELLIGENCE (AI) FITS INTO ALL THIS

Artificial intelligence is an imitation of human intelligence in the form of machines like computers.

HOW AI IS APPLIED BY BANKS TO PREVENT FRAUD AND PROTECT YOU

Now that we have discussed the many things that you need to be aware of to protect yourself from fraud, let me give you some comfort in the fact that even though fraudsters exist and are constantly taking chances to keep up with change, it doesn't mean that one must completely avoid transacting, especially digitally. Digital transactions are the future and we need to move in this direction as the world is embracing it. I have observed that there are still many people out there who have a phobia of transacting digitally because they fear falling victim to fraud. The sad part about this is that the cost of transacting physically is a waste of time and money. Have you ever noticed that a bank deposit fee costs more than an internet transfer fee? Have you ever noticed that travelling to a clothing store to pay your pay your monthly instalment incurs travel costs and requires patience and time to stand in long queues?

- Banks and other financial institutions apply the use of artificial intelligence to understand and distinguish between normal and abnormal behaviours of individuals when transacting. Therefore, by this distinction, they apply AI to detect when any abnormal behaviour occurs on an account belonging to one of their customers. This is enabled by data tracking through record keeping of an individual's normal behaviour. When an unusual or "abnormal" transaction takes place on an account, the financial institution is likely to contact the owner of the account to verify whether they are aware of the transaction.
- Some fraud can be detected instantly, in real-time.

Institutions have embraced the use of models to detect real-time fraud and can then immediately contact the account holder to verify if they are the ones transacting.
- Institutions make use of analysts who constantly improve and refine these models in order to keep up with the moving trends of all types of fraud and abnormal transactions.

There is a lot that financial institutions do these days to protect their customers. So, even if it seems risky to embrace digital transacting, you can be assured that the major financial intuitions are totally committed to keeping your money safe.

Chapter Nine

LESSON 9

NEW PROFESSIONALS SHOULD AVOID BAD BEGINNINGS

It's always easier to keep up good habits if you start from the beginning.

As soon as you start to earn any form of income, you become potential profit to any form of business that offers credit or financial services. The nature of business for companies that offer credit/loans is to lend out money, and in doing so, earn their profit from interest.

FINANCIAL SERVICES COME WITH A COST

Like any business that provides service, the aim is to make profit, so there is always a cost involved for the service.

It is wise therefore, to always keep this in mind when you receive a call, e-mail or SMS offering you a loan. All these offers come with a service that you pay for. We understand that every business needs to make a profit to survive and keep the economy going, but some institutions become greedy and some, or all of their service fees, become overpriced. Before applying for a loan, always check to make sure that the institution has your best interests at heart and that their values are innovatively driven and customer centric. Innovations within the financial services industry have lead, over the years, to the introduction of new digital solutions that cut your total costs for financial services. For example, there are costs you may not even think about, or be aware of, such as paying for transport to go to a bank to sign a loan offer. These costs are outside of your loan agreement, but they still form part of your total expenditure for that loan.

As we are trying to create generational wealth for our children, we should be aware of opportunistic institutions that offer us massive debts without special consideration, just for the sake of making profit.

NOW LET'S BEGIN AT THE BEGINNING!

Every situation that exists in this world has a pattern which forms its existence. Whether the situation is good or bad, the design and consistency of the pattern defines the outcome, or current condition of the situation.

Many people end up paying huge interest rates and charges because their beginnings were not good.

This chapter is dedicated to all the young people who will one day have financial responsibilities and will most likely have to, at some stage; borrow money to fulfil their responsibilities, dreams or goals.

Micro-lenders are constantly sourcing information about people to whom they can sell debt. The loans they offer can be tempting, especially because their lending policies are not as strict as those of the more highly regulated financial service providers.

For example, it is difficult to regulate loan-sharks in that they operate outside of formal infrastructure and so are able to take advantage of people. Some micro-lenders tend to operate like loan-sharks, as they too don't get as much attention in the form of regulation, as the big financial institutions do. These lenders can make your financial life miserable for eternity!

Sometimes things just go sour from the beginning and in a financial sense, bad beginnings can be a huge burden you may need to carry for a very long time.

A GOOD EXAMPLE OF BAD BEGINNINGS

In the year 2006, I worked in a call centre doing debt collections, which is how I met a guy by the name of Siyanda, who was a Chartered Accountant at the time. Siyanda was heavily in debt. As I recall, he had three clothing accounts, eight different micro-loans, a vehicle loan, as well as three furniture and homeware accounts.

The first thing that struck me about Siyanda was that although he was a qualified Chartered Accountant, and was therefore earning big bucks, he was struggling to meet his obligations. His accounts fell under my portfolio, so my job was to try to get hold of him to discuss his arrears and to conclude arrangements for him to pay his debts. I tried continuously for several months. Some days he would pick up the phone but as soon as he realised that I was calling from a debt collection agency, he would make an excuse like, "I'm about to go into a meeting, please call me back," and then would not pick up the phone when I called again.

Days, weeks and months went by, until one day I called him using a more casual tone. I didn't make it obvious that I was phoning from a formal organisation but greeted him as I would a friend and then asked for ten minutes of his time. He agreed. I had managed to make him comfortable by attempting to figure out his frustrations.

As I said before, Siyanda was heavily in debt. I also mentioned that I had fifteen of his accounts on my portfolio, accounts that had been handed over to our company to collect on the arrears. I found out that that was just the tip of the iceberg.

As Siyanda explained his frustrations to me he opened my eyes even wider. He disclosed to me that besides owing on those fifteen accounts, he had more debt of which I was not aware and that he was also in arrears with those other creditors.

He further explained to me that he didn't want to ignore my calls but had desperately, and unsuccessfully, been trying to figure a way out of the mess that he was in.

The situation was too bad! He was beyond repair!

Some debt problems are curable provided that the debtor is vigilant and responsible enough to identify and acknowledge early enough that he/she is in trouble. The problem with Siyanda was that he enjoyed all the attention he was getting from the micro-lenders too much.

Siyanda had bad beginnings because as soon as he started earning an income he received tremendous attention from these micro-lenders. This attention blinded him to such an extent that as soon as his salary was spent, he would be tempted to use credit from the micro-loans that he was continuously offered from all corners.

Here's what went wrong with Siyanda:

He earned good money but didn't limit his spending according to his income. In his head, the credit that he received from the micro-lenders was part of his cash-flow and more like a monthly supplement to his income.

He got to a stage where he was surviving solely on debt. His lifestyle ended up becoming totally misaligned from his real income and because of this, especially as it happened at the beginning of his career, he destroyed a whole lot of things in his life; things such as his budget and his credit score, which in turn made all of his dreams and goals impossible to achieve.

After all this, what does he do when he realises that he has accumulated too much debt? He chooses to ignore communications from debt collectors.

One important lesson can be learned from the tragedy of Siyanda's life. Once you get used to subsidising your day to day living with borrowed money, you are very likely to end up in an endless loop of micro-lending.

Siyanda landed in this loop because of a lack of education in basic finance management. From the beginning he failed to implement a budget. He took one loan after another without assessing whether he could afford all his repayments within the confines of his income and in the end, he was forced to subsidise his income from micro-loans just to survive.

HOW TO AVOID BAD BEGINNINGS

- Before applying for credit on a banking product with which you are not familiar, ask for information about how they work. Information such as interest rate charges and the rules applicable to the loan repayment. If possible, get advice from people you know who currently, or have previously, made use of the same product.
- Don't get too excited by the fact that you are now employed and earning a monthly income, and are most likely getting attention from countless lenders offering you loans. Getting involved with some of these institutions is not good for you. This is why it is important to form a good relationship with your Bank. Be aware that a large majority of the products that are offered by dodgy lenders are likely to be offered by the recognised banks and also that it would be cheaper to obtain and retain those products if you already have a good relationship with your bank.
- Always monitor the ratio between your income and your expenses.
- Track the patterns that lead to various outcomes in your life. For every situation there is a pattern which forms its structure/design. One of the most recognisable reasons for ending up over-indebted is the pattern of reckless borrowing. By reckless borrowing I mean someone who takes up credit without fitting it properly into his budget.

- Learn from the mistakes others make.

Siyanda merely represented profit gain to all the many companies that offered him credit: nothing more, nothing less. He gave up his lending power to them, thereby enabling them to profit from his failure to pay attention to, and ultimately alter, his pattern of reckless borrowing and spending. This habit of taking up micro-loans managed to ruin not only his credit score but also his reputation. Inevitably, this is what happens when you survive from month to month only because of micro-loans.

In the end, Siyanda's biggest downfall was that he had no understanding of financial literacy, even though he was an accountant.

Chapter Ten

LESSON 10

CHOOSE YOUR DEBTS WISELY

Have a valid purpose for every debt.

Borrowing is an essential part of life for most people. In basic terms, borrowing is a way of getting help from someone who has the means to help, but it comes at a price because of the risk attached, arising from the probability that what's borrowed might not be returned to its owner.

Therefore, as borrowing comes at a price, it is vital to make rules as to what can be borrowed and for what reasons, how much can be borrowed (limits) and when to borrow.

WHAT CAN BE BORROWED AND FOR WHAT REASONS?

A valid reason to incur debt may be to purchase, or invest in, an asset. Another reason you may need to borrow is for emergencies where immediate or urgent payment is required.

Assets not only increase our net worth but can also be essential parts of our lives, assets like a house, a car, furniture, or even business equipment. These can be very expensive to purchase with cash, which is why most people have to borrow to purchase them.

> Borrow to invest in an asset or for an emergency. At least try to make this your number one rule. It will save you the trouble of paying unnecessary fees.

Always make sure however, that the assets for which you borrow are evaluated properly to ensure that they are worth the cost of the credit and also so that you are totally satisfied that they will last long enough to serve their purpose. For example, it is not wise to purchase, as an asset, a car which is beyond its lifespan and that will incur further expense to repair and maintain.

Some people go to the extent of taking out a personal loan to buy an older car, reason being that a vehicle finance company is unlikely to finance the car for reasons which might include the fact that the car is way beyond its life span.

It is important to note that unless you can afford to pay cash for an asset like a car, it should be purchased using credit that is specifically designed for it. The reason for this comes down to the risk attached. The risk a creditor takes, in that he may lose all the money lent to you, is offset by the asset. So, should you for some reason be unable to pay your debt on the car, the lender can recover the asset and sell it.

Property is financed via a mortgage loan, which is specifically designed in a different way. It caters for many aspects such as the loan period and a reasonable long term interest rate. The repayment term for a mortgage loan, obtained from a reputable bank, is typically set between twenty and thirty years and the interest rate charged is usually much less than that of a personal loan or any dodgy loan from an unauthorised financial service provider. The reason for this is also because this type of loan is for purchasing an asset and the risk attached is reduced by the fact that there is collateral/security in the immovable property (the house) which can be sold should you fail to maintain payments on the loan.

BORROW WITH A VISION AND A PLAN

When you borrow a large sum of money, it is vital to have a plan in place as to how you are going to pay off the loan, especially if something goes wrong. You should not rely solely on the fact that you initially have a steady income.

Your plan of repayment should try to account for as many events that might possibly interrupt or negatively affect your repayments, as possible. Also, try to stay away from solutions such as pawning your goods for money, as the interest they charge at most pawn shops is too high. Why should you open yourself up to further interest charges when you have already provided security that should cover the loan amount?

Make sure that you calculate the total cost of the debt: according to the NCR, a creditor must disclose the total cost of the debt. The total cost will include details such as your interest rate, admin fee, initiation fee, total interest sum calculated over the full repayment term, and other details like insurance. If, once you have the full information, you find that the repayment will be too much for you, you still have the right to ask for cancellation of the loan as long as you haven't signed the agreement.

QUESTIONS THAT COULD TRIGGER YOUR VISION

- When am I likely to finish paying the debt?
- Is my budget able to accommodate this new loan agreement?
- What is the total estimated interest amount that I would pay over the loan period/term? When taking out a loan, the creditor is required to disclose this amount to you on the credit agreement. If you feel that this portion is too high for you, then you still have the option to cancel the loan before signing the agreement. It is important to note however, that as the amount is calculated on your initial agreed interest amount, it may be subject to national

> interest rate changes by the reserve bank if the rate is not
> fixed.
- What valuable things will I gain from this loan, or how will
  this loan improve my life?

LIFE EVENTS THAT NEED PLANNING

School Fees and expenses

At the beginning of every year, over-and-above basic school fees, parents are expected to spend a lot of money on uniforms, books and stationary for their school-going children. It would therefore be unwise to take out a temporary loan in December which has a due date in January. A temporary (temp) loan is expected to be paid within a thirty day period, thus the due date is exactly thirty days after acquiring the loan. So if you take this loan in December, knowing that in January you have school fees to pay, chances are that you are going to have financial difficulties in the month of January as you will have too many commitments.

Throughout my years in the debt collections space, I found that the primary reason for people being in arrears was simply because they were over-committed.

Once you are in the position of being over-committed, the chances are likely that you will miss one or more instalments and then it starts becoming difficult to get back to a clean slate.

Retrenchment

If you are aware that your employer is considering retrenchments, it would be unwise to continue borrowing. Often, long before a company begins the process of retrenchment, there are rumours that such might be happening. But even with this knowledge, there are people who bury their heads in the sand and believe that if it happens it's going to happen to someone else, thereby ignoring the fact that they themselves also face the risk of losing their jobs. Living in a dream world, they continue to borrow and a few months down the line when they get retrenched, they find themselves having to choose which of their debts they can manage to pay with their UIF or pension funds. Being in this position may also cost you future employment opportunities, as now you will be in debt and most companies these days check your credit profile to see if you are in good standing before employing you, especially financial institutions. It wouldn't make sense, for example, for a financial institution to hire a financial advisor who is struggling to handle their own personal finances.

Maternity

When you are planning for, or find out that you are expecting a baby, make sure that you fully understand your employer's maternity leave policy. Employers offer different maternity remuneration packages at their own discretion. Some may pay 75% of your salary for four months whereas others may only pay 50% for three months. You will need to plan carefully how to cover any existing debts, as well as any new expenses you may incur during pregnancy, as well for the birth of your baby and afterward.

Salary increases

Now this can be a tricky one. Many people, when approaching the time for their annual salary increase, incur debts in the hope that the increase, and/or expected bonus, will cover the repayment of the debts. Never take up new debt before you receive confirmation of your new package or know exactly what increase/bonus you will be getting.

Retirement

Although being over-indebted may be the most prevalent reason for people to be in arrears on their loans, some people are in that position because they continued to take loans too close to their retirement. If you know that you will take retirement at the age of 60, it is impractical and irresponsible to take a loan with a five year repayment term when you turn 58. This will give you only two years to pay up that loan while you are still employed, or that you will be using your pension for three years to continue making payment. Chances are high that you may no longer be employable at that age and you may then end up stressing about debts. No-one wants to be in a position where they are forced to use their hard earned pension money to pay debts and possibly be left with nothing. Becoming a financial burden on your children is not a nice thing, especially if they are just starting their own lives and trying to establish their own budgets.

Death and other emergencies

In life, bad things happen: accidents happen, people get sick and people die.

It is therefore wise to try and prepare for these events as much as possible, as they usually cost a lot and you don't want to be in a position where you are forced to take out a loan or borrow money.

A good way to prepare for emergencies, or events that we didn't anticipate, is to take out insurance policies.

- Avoid borrowing money to bury your loved ones. Get a funeral policy.
- Avoid borrowing money to fix your car due to accidents. Get vehicle insurance.
- Avoid borrowing money to buy new furniture after a home break-in or damage from a burst geyser. Get household insurance.

There are many different insurances policies, catering for specific needs that you can use to protect yourself. Having insurance becomes very useful to protect you from borrowing money to cover the situation.

The importance of saving

Preparing for emergencies is a fundamental reason to put away 20% of your monthly income as savings. If you have a substantial amount of money saved up, it may not be necessary to borrow for an emergency.

Having the security of insurance and savings helps a lot in the long run as you are less likely to find yourself in a place of desperation where you are willing to take up any form of loan to get yourself out of an emergency situation, even if the terms for that loan are unfair.

CLOSING WORDS

Everything in its purpose, time and place! Life is not short; it's too long, especially if you make wrong decisions that haunt you for a lifetime.

Everything in its purpose – Get the correct loan for the correct purpose and not merely to support your lifestyle. A loan should never be a top-up to your income.

Everything in its time – If it's not a good time for you to borrow, don't borrow. Rather try to sell possessions that you no longer need, to get cash.

Everything in its place – Any type of loan that you take should align with its use. A vehicle loan is designed to cater for the purpose of purchasing a vehicle and therefore the interest rate on it should be lower than that of a personal loan. Temp loans are supposed to be once-off and temporary, not a recurring thing that you take up each month. For example, note that the interest and initiation fees that you will pay on these loans on a monthly basis would cause a huge financial setback for you, even though you may not realise it. Just try to calculate all the initiation fees and interest that would be applied should you be taking up a temp loan each month for a year.

Is my life going to be short, or too long?

I've asked myself this question many times and, even though we may not all do this in the same fashion; I know that we all consider the duration of our existence in this world to some extent. Life may at times seem too short when we think of our dreams and the things we want to accomplish and experience, but it can also seem too long if we measure it through our experiences of discomfort and pain.

Ultimately, we must think before we do. Especially before we make commitments to take up loans that are not good for us. The experience that follows may cause financial distress even beyond your lifetime and affect the lives of your children, and this is not a legacy anyone wishes to leave behind.

Chapter Eleven

LESSON 11

RETRENCHMENT & MAKING USE OF UIF AND PENSIONS

Things you had yesterday might be gone today because everything that has a beginning also has an end, unfortunately. Sometimes in life, we find ourselves facing this reality and having to deal with it. Some endings come at a time where we are at least prepared for it, while others come too soon, at a time when we least expect them.

I would like to take this opportunity to extend my condolences to everyone who has recently lost loved ones, and especially those who have lost loved ones during the COVID-19 pandemic. Dealing with the harsh reality of having to let go of someone, or even something, you deeply value is extremely difficult, especially when your loss comes at an unexpected time. As I mentioned at the beginning of this book in the dedication section, I too unexpectedly lost someone very dear to me: my wonderful mother, Martha Mafa Thwala, so I can understand exactly how hard it is to cope with loss.

UIF

The UIF, also known as the short term unemployment insurance fund, comes in very handy in the following events:

- When your employment is terminated by your employer, e.g. retrenchment;
- Maternity or adoption leave;
- When you are unable to work due to serious illness.

UIF is however not available to people who;

- Are unemployed due to resignation;
- Have been suspended from work;
- Have absconded from work.

CONTRIBUTION SCALES

- The current contribution amount from your salary while you are employed is 1% of your annual remuneration and is paid in monthly increments.
- In addition, your employer contributes an amount totalling 1% of your annual remuneration on your behalf, and thus submits a total of 2% for the premium of the insurance.

Employers who may need more information and guidance regarding UIF payments may contact SARS www.sars.gov.za for assistance.

You can make use of www.ufiling.co.za/uif either as an employer or employee to register or submit a claim.

A tip from my side for employees: if you are unsure whether you have been registered for UIF, verify this by contacting the labour department.

CLAIMS

Claims may be submitted to the labour office, either in person or online via the website above.

Thank you to all the employers who have diligently contributed towards UIF for their employees. Your accountability has made a huge difference in people's lives.

On behalf the people of South Africa, I would also like to extend gratitude to those citizens who have been reliable in paying their taxes and to those who have made donations to help the country survive during this global crisis. Our heartfelt thanks also, to the many international institutions that have extended their help. The country is truly grateful.

RAMAPHOSA ANNOUNCES R500-BILLION COVID-19 PACKAGE FOR SOUTH AFRICA

By Beauregard Tromp Sipho Kings 21 Apr 2020

Speaking to the nation on Tuesday night, President Cyril Ramaphosa announced an "extraordinary coronavirus budget" adding up to R500-billion to be injected into the economy.

The funding will come from internal sources, such as the Unemployment Insurance Fund (UIF), and Ramaphosa said discussions had begun with international financial institutions, such as the World Bank and International Monetary Fund (IMF).

The R500-billion makes up 10% of the national gross domestic product (GDP).

Health will receive priority, with the poor and most vulnerable catered for in a range of measures that include an increase in the social grant and billions of rands in subsidies for business and wages.

Ramaphosa started his address from the Union Buildings in Pretoria, saying: "It has demanded of you great fortitude and endurance … required great sacrifice. I salute you and thank you." The national lockdown, now into its 26th day, had given the government space to save "tens of thousands of lives".

"Our foremost priority is health interventions, and to save lives," he said, adding that R20-billion would go to financing the healthcare response.

With 3 465 confirmed positive Covid-19 tests and 58 deaths, Ramaphosa reiterated the government's position that South Africa is still in the early stages of the pandemic and that this would last for the "foreseeable future".

The economic package is the third phase of the government's strategy, with the president saying the "pandemic requires an economic response that is equal to the scale of disruption it is causing".

The first phases included tax relief, wage support, funding for small business and a disaster release fund. The initial phases have been heavily criticised for not putting enough support into the economy, as business shut down and people lost their jobs.

The third phase will involve big-money interventions in the economy, ranging from a substantial infrastructure build to speedy implementation of economic reform and transformation of the economy. Ramaphosa was light on details for these sweeping plans but promised that the government would "outline this in the days to come".

To create the R500-billion plan, Ramaphosa said he had met with business, community, labour, premiers, mayors and MECs. Cabinet had then considered various proposals that would boost health spending, bring relief from hunger, support companies, help people in social distress and help with a phased reopening of the economy.

Of the R500-billion proposed economic stimulus, R130-billion will come from a reprioritisation of the current budget, with the rest of the funds to be raised from local sources, including the

UIF, as well as from global partners and international finance institutions that have worked on financing packages to assist countries to address the effects of the coronavirus.

The biggest part of the R500-billion would be a R200-billion loan guarantee scheme, in partnership with major banks, the treasury and the South African Reserve Bank. This, Ramaphosa said, would help to pay salaries and suppliers. The scheme is open to companies with a turnover of less than R300-million a year and would support about 700 000 firms and three million employees.

R20-billion will be allocated to municipalities for emergency water supplies, public transport, food and shelter for homeless people. The president noted that in only a few weeks the number of people plunged into poverty and suffering food insecurity had risen dramatically. R20-billion has also been set aside for the relief of hunger and social distress.

The South African Social Security Agency (Sassa) will also begin implementing a technology-based solution to roll out food assistance on scale through vouchers to ensure assistance reaches people faster.

R40-billion has also been set aside for income support for workers whose employers are unable to pay their staff.

A further R100-billion will be set aside for the protection of jobs, as well as to create jobs.

The finer details of all these plans would be shared in an adjusted budget, which would be shared by the minister of finance.

Commenting on the historic economic recovery plan, Ramaphosa said the country and the world would never be the same, but that his ambition was that we forged a new economy with greater equality.

He finished by saying he would address the nation again on Thursday on "measures that will be taken beyond the nationwide lockdown to reopen the economy".

MY HUMBLE REQUEST TO EMPLOYERS

The advent of Covid-19 has taught us that nothing in life is guaranteed and at the same time has highlighted the fact that anything can come to an end at any time. Now is the time to learn from these unfortunate events and begin to prioritise the needs of the people who dedicate the majority of their waking lives to working for you, and more especially to assist those workers who qualify for the benefits as governed by the **Unemployment Insurance Act of 2001** and the **Unemployment Insurance Contribution Act of 2002,** but due to lack of knowledge or neglect are currently not covered under this insurance.

Even the above article, published by The Mail & Guardian, states clearly that some of the funding for Covid-19 relief comes from internal sources such as the UIF.

It is also time for the education system to include basic financial literacy in the school curriculums to make people aware of benefits such as UIF from an early age. It's time for educators of financial literacy to become pro-active rather than re-active so that we can avoid situations in the future where people only learn of things that might have assisted them through bad times, when it is too late. It is also time to encourage the people who may have qualified for assistance but did not receive it to come forward to get justice for these oversights.

Recently, I have come across many employed people who fit the requirements but were not aware of it. Most of these included, but were not limited to the following: taxi drivers, domestic workers and shop assistants. In this time of crisis, these people are sitting at home, unable to work to earn an income and thereby struggling to cater for their basic needs, or even feed themselves and their loved ones, due to the restrictions placed by government as safety measures against Covid-19. Some of these people could have benefitted from UIF grants but have not, and this is due solely to a lack of knowledge.

If those of us who have an understanding of these things, would take up the responsibility of teaching basic financial literacy to the less fortunate, it would make a major difference in the lives of many families, and less children would go to sleep with hungry stomachs. If employers could show more foresight and empathy towards not only their businesses, but also the financial wellbeing of their employees, perhaps those employees who lose their jobs are more likely to survive the depression. Perhaps domestic violence would decrease. Maybe even the general crime rate would come down.

It will take a long time, if ever, for things to get better, should we continue to turn a blind eye to these problems, instead of trying to fix them by empowering people with basic financial knowledge.

MAKING USE OF PENSION FUNDS UPON RETRENCHMENT

Pension funds are savings which are built up during your employable years for when you reach retirement age and are no longer able to work. These are long term savings plans which generally qualify for tax relief, in that a portion of the money that an employee would have paid to the government for tax goes into the pension fund. It forms part of the deductions from your total salary.

In the event that you are retrenched, look at the following options. The cashing in of pension or provident funds is not advised. My intention, however, is not to give advice but merely to share information which I think may be useful. In any situation, where you are cornered and need to make a sound decision regarding your options but are unable to do so without assistance, you should consult with a qualified financial advisor.

OPTIONS

Although a primary function of the pension fund is to provide an income when a person retires, employees are given the option to withdraw a lump-sum amount from the fund as a retrenchment benefit or even if they just resign.

WITHDRAWAL OF ALL THE AVAILABLE FUNDS

Some people choose to withdraw the all the money that is due to them, even though they are aware that it might not be a good thing to use money intended as savings for the future when they are old and no longer working. If you choose to withdraw the full amount, the first R500 000.00 of your retrenchment benefit is tax free; any amount over R500 000.00 will be taxed according to the rules and rates that apply to you as per the tax tables. This tax benefit is only available, however, provided that you have never utilised it before, i.e. from a previous employer. It's a once in a life time R500 000.00 benefit. If you have used, or qualified for, a tax-free withdrawal in the past, calculations will be applied to determine the tax-free portion.

AVAILABLE OPTIONS FOR PRESERVING THE FUND

- Another option is to preserve the fund by leaving it in the existing retirement fund investment portfolio and allowing the balance to continue to grow. Once you obtain new employment, you can then opt to transfer the funds to their retirement plan.
- You can also opt to withdraw a portion and leave the balance in the existing fund. Some people opt to withdraw a small portion and leave the remainder to grow, if they still have not made use of the R500 000.00 tax free benefit.
- Another possible choice is to transfer the funds to a retirement annuity. This is a good option if you want to ensure that no funds can be withdrawn until retirement age, generally at around age 55-62.

IMPORTANT TO REMEMBER

When deciding what to do with your retirement funds, always look carefully at your circumstances and remember to refer to the brainstorming of your financial goals. Yes, the goals and objectives as discussed at the beginning of this book. This will help you to identify the crucial things necessary for your financial and overall wellbeing.

Chapter Twelve

LESSON 12

MONEY AND EMOTIONAL INTELLIGENCE

WHAT IS EMOTIONAL INTELLIGENCE?

When we speak of emotional intelligence, we refer to the capacity of an individual to manage his/her emotions and the emotions of other people.

THE MIRROR!

A strange concept became stuck in my mind long ago at school, when my grade 6 history teacher was explaining to us how people used to trade goods before money was widely introduced. I was shocked! What I couldn't understand was how people could exchange valuable goods such as land, livestock, or any other essential resource, for glitter (a mirror).

Now think about the present: do people still exchange valuable resources for glitter?

Not as much anymore. Over the years people have collected knowledge and understanding (logic) that enables them to differentiate between things that have value and things that are worthless, or have less value.

And yet, people are still at times tricked into overspending due to emotion. To overpower these emotions, you need strong logic! Logic is the reason people are less likely to exchange more for less.

IT'S IMPORTANT FOR YOU TO KNOW THE FOLLOWING

WHAT CONTROLS YOUR BRAIN?

The study of psychology suggests that the brain is controlled by two components, the rational side and the emotional side.

1. Emotional side – Controls feelings and imagination.

The people that were trading items of intrinsic value for glitter were taken over by emotion. But you can't expect that people living in these days to be quite as gullible because now most people transact based on logic, not just on emotion. They verify facts, no matter how shiny the item of exchange might be.

2. The Rational side – Which is about logic (reasoning and validity).

People these days are guided by logic to do fair transactions. The glitter no longer matters as much; it's the value and the usefulness of the item that matters more.

Through knowledge and understanding, people manage to transact based on logic and thus validate the worth of each and every transaction, or every exchange of goods and services, that they conduct. People have mastered the art of estimating the exchange offer based on the product, service or reward offered for the trade.

IMPROVING RATIONALITY FOR THE SAKE OF YOUR WEALTH

Another thing that you need to know is that some of your emotions come from stereotypes. Stereotypes influence emotions; they paint a picture which affects your logic and reasoning.

Stereotypes are just oversimplified conceptions, perceptions, opinions, or beliefs about a group, race, individual, or thing.

Example: "I will never allow my child to attend a government school because private schools offer better education." There is no fact or logic to support this statement. It may be a perception that comes from the fact that private schools charge higher school fees, which might make one think, or expect, that the education offered in a private school is superior.

The lack of financial literacy has also played a huge role in our lives and often causes us to make decisions based on emotions and stereotypes.

LOOKING BACK ON PREVIOUS LESSONS IN THIS BOOK: SOME DANGERS OF ACTING ON EMOTION AND HOW IT AFFECTS YOUR FINANCIAL FREEDOM

Each time you make a decision you are faced with two things, emotion and logic. It's up to you which one you will choose.

Looking back over everything we have discussed, from budgeting, credit scores, debts, and fraud, to the future of banking and many more, everything comes down to a choice between logic and emotion.

1. People with weaker emotional intelligence are more likely to deviate from their budget rules.
2. With weak emotions overruling their logic, some people take up debts on behalf of friends and family who cannot qualify for credit and in the end these people get burned. But then what else could you expect for taking up credit for someone who doesn't qualify? When I worked with Home Loans collections in the bank, I came across many cases where people had applied for home loans on behalf of their

girlfriends, family members or even friends. Inevitably, after a certain period, the people that they took credit for started defaulting on their payments. As the bank can only hold the person, or persons, with whom they are in contract liable for payment, this negatively affected the people who took out the loan. Often the bank consultant/collector would hear stories that the bondholder was waiting for their ex-girlfriend or brother to send them money to make payment, as it was them for whom they had taken up the loan. It was sad to hear such things, because in the end the bank was often forced to recover their money via the legal route, and so the good Samaritans lost their creditworthiness due to emotional decisions to help out the people close to them.

3. Because lack of knowledge can increase fear, people might be too scared to convert to self-help banking. Many people are not confident in using digital banking because they fear that they might become victims of fraud, but if they took the time to be educated on how to use the application, they could limit their chances of being defrauded and enjoy the benefits of digital banking.

4. Fraudsters and scammers take advantage of your emotions and in so doing, steal your money by deceiving you. Due to your emotional vulnerability, they deceive you into thinking that you have achieved what you would most like to achieve and make you believe in what you see in front of you, as you fail to validate the facts or follow logic.

5. When you are desperate, dodgy micro-lenders and loan-sharks can play on your emotions by making you think that you are still financially fit enough to obtain loans, knowing that you will be paying them excessive amounts of interest.

6. We discussed an accountant who found himself in a debt loop. Even though he was a qualified professional, interest and collection fees were steadily accumulating on his debts and he had no idea where to even begin to sort out his issues. He was ruled by fear - another case of weak

emotional intelligence! He was overwhelmed by his debt and didn't know how to approach his creditors to ask for help. If he had used logic from the beginning, he may have been able to acquire the help he needed before the situation became desperate.

7. Emotions can make your wants seem like needs. Everybody wants to go for a holiday in Mauritius, but some people might convince themselves that this want is a need, and they come up with many reasons to make it into a need.

Things like:

- My divorce was tough, so I need a holiday in Mauritius.

- It was a rough year for me, so now I need to party hard.

- My child passed matric, so I need to take her to Mauritius for a holiday.

Emotional control becomes vital as we grow up. You can do further research and read many articles online that can help you to improve your emotional intelligence and control.

The relationship between financial stability and health

Many people are not aware that there is another aspect of health that is vital for their overall wellbeing, that aspect is financial fitness.

If we are not well emotionally, we may end up with unhealthy conditions like depression, stress, heart problems, and so on, which left untreated, could eventually lead to death. Lack of proper financial fitness can cause the same emotional reactions and physical manifestations.

Therefore, being financially healthy is as vital as being physically and emotionally healthy.

CONCLUSION

Financial literacy is a broad subject, not limited to only the things discussed in this book. I have tried to address the issues I observed throughout my career, with which most people struggle and repeatedly fail at, but I don't want you to limit your attention or knowledge only to them. Don't be afraid to find ways to constantly expand your knowledge and then share what you have learnt with other people, as passing on knowledge and winning behaviours, especially to the younger generations, is very rewarding. The thing that troubles me the most is that too many people have to learn about finances from negative experiences.

Most important of all the lessons in this book is emotional intelligence. A majority of plans succeed, not only through staying power (persistence) but also by developing strong emotional intelligence.

Weak emotional intelligence can make one lose focus on the important things, especially when situations are out of control and overwhelming such as the tough times we are living in now.

———

Without strong emotional intelligence:

- You will not have the ability to define solid goals and objectives
- You will struggle to be strict with your budgeting
- You might be too discouraged to fix your credit score when it's damaged, or find it difficult to keep it in good standing
- You may find it difficult to refuse the temptation of taking up debt unnecessarily
- You may find yourself without a home, owing huge debts or find yourself in various financial difficulties due the fear of asking for assistance from qualified people
- Fraudsters may find you an easy target
- You might find it hard to embrace the use of technology in transacting.

A majority of people all over the world are heavily bruised by the consequences of COVID-19. If you find it hard to stay balanced, you always have the option to make use of professional help to restore emotional balance and a good state of mind.

There are many external factors that might impact your financial wellness, so it is wise to constantly keep yourself informed of new trends and changes. It is important to keep track of things such as interest rate changes, laws and regulations governing tax reductions, pension funds, transaction charges, technology improvements and new trending scams. It helps to subscribe to services that deliver news addressing such issues.

We have now reached the end of this book. I hope that you enjoyed reading it and that you learned something valuable in the process.

I would also like to wish you all the best with your endeavours towards success.

REFERENCES

LIST OF REFERENCES

1. https://mg.co.za/article/2020-04-21-ramaphosa-announces-r500-billion-covid-19-package-for-south-africa/
2. https://www.justice.gov.za/legislation/acts/1998-114.pdf
3. http://www.pasa.org.za/resources/debicheck
4. https://www.transunion.co.za/product/credit-report-and-score?channel=paid&cid=ppc:google:GBTransunionCreditScore&gclid=EAIaIQobChMIo_rx5dzt6wIVGO7tCh2i7A2tEAAYASAAEgLj8PD_BwE